Behind Enemy Lines

Book One

EDEN

How the Serpent Still Speaks

Joshua M. Sells, Esq., J.D., LL.M.

Legacy Builders Press

ISBN: 979-8-9931446-7-2

Published by Legacy Builders Press
Printed in the United States of America

For permissions, contact: books@legacybuilderspress.org

Scripture quotations are from the King James Bible.

ABOUT THE AUTHOR

Joshua Sells brings a unique blend of professional expertise and personal testimony to his writing. He holds a Juris Doctor from Case Western Reserve University and an LL.M. in Taxation from Georgetown University Law Center. Over the course of his career, Josh has worked for two of the Big Four global consulting firms, advised Fortune 500 companies in complex mergers and acquisitions, and built a reputation as a trusted voice in the world of tax law. He has owned and led several businesses, and today he serves as the founder of a national tax law firm dedicated to "fighting the IRS" on behalf of individuals and small businesses.

Yet, for all of the titles, credentials, and worldly success, Josh discovered that none of it could satisfy the deepest need of his heart. Though outwardly accomplished, he inwardly wrestled with emptiness, discontentment, and striving. In 2018, Josh came to saving faith in Jesus Christ, and in 2021, he surrendered his life fully to Him. That moment of surrender reframed everything. His career, his ambition, and even his past successes found their rightful place under the Lordship of Christ.

Josh and his wife, Kailley, live in northeast Ohio where they are raising their seven children with the prayerful goal of passing on a Christ-centered legacy. Their home is a place of family discipleship, daily devotion, and the joyful chaos of life with a large family. Together, they faithfully serve at their local church, Community Baptist Temple, where they are actively involved in ministry and outreach. Josh's greatest desire is not that readers see his résumé, but that they see the grace of God that reached down into a driven, ambitious heart and brought lasting fulfillment.

In August 2025, Josh answered God's call to full-time ministry in evangelism, being sent out of Community Baptist Temple. Out of that call, Legacy Builders Press was born—not just as a publishing effort, but as a preaching, teaching, and writing ministry dedicated to proclaiming God's truth. Its mission is to provide biblically faithful preaching, resources, and books that equip believers to leave a Christ-centered legacy and to lift high the name of Jesus for generations to come. Through Legacy Builders Press, Josh writes to encourage others to build their lives on what truly matters—not on fleeting success, but on the eternal hope found in Christ.

"The greatest legacy I can leave my children is not my career or accomplishments, but a life surrendered to Jesus Christ. He alone satisfies, and He alone is worthy."

TABLE OF CONTENTS

MY TESTIMONY – AND HOW YOU CAN KNOW CHRIST TOO

I was raised in a Baptist church from a young age. My parents were faithful to bring me to services, and I grew up hearing the Bible preached. As a boy of eight or nine, I had already "made a profession of faith" and been baptized. I had said the sinner's prayer, but looking back, I realize I didn't truly understand salvation or my own need for it.

One Wednesday night as a kid, I remember feeling a deep, unshakable conviction after the service. I tried to avoid everyone, even hiding behind my mom. My parents knew it was something spiritual and suggested I talk to my grandma Betty—a godly woman who walked with Christ. Pride kept me from it. I thought I could handle things on my own. That pride would follow me for years.

At fourteen, I made another profession of faith at teen camp. Not long after, my parents stopped going to church, and I did too. Through high school and into college, I drifted from God. Later, I got involved again in church life—serving, attending faithfully—but I was never at peace about my salvation. Whenever an evangelist preached on eternity, I'd feel a surge of fear that if I died that night, I might not go to heaven.

Many nights I prayed privately, "Lord, if I'm not saved, save me." But nothing changed. I was embarrassed to admit my doubts to anyone. What would people think? That fear and pride kept me silent.

Then in 2018, my pastor, Mark O'Donnell, shared his own testimony. He said, "The devil may tempt you to doubt your salvation, but he'll never tempt you to get saved." That truth hit me hard. Why would the devil urge me to come forward in a church service? That was God's call, not Satan's. I realized I wasn't saved, and my pride was the barrier.

On Monday, I emailed my pastor asking to meet—partly so I couldn't talk myself out of it. By Wednesday night, I was ready. I knew all the Bible verses. I knew the gospel. But this time, I came empty-handed—no pride, no self-sufficiency, no terms of my own—just surrender to Christ. That night in August 2018, I trusted Him fully, and I have never doubted since.

It wasn't until later that I fully surrendered my life to the Lord, but my day of salvation was August 2018. Whether I only thought I was saved before as a child or truly was, I know this: that night I made an adult decision as an adult, and *everything changed.*

The Good News of the Gospel

Friend, maybe you've grown up in church. Maybe you've prayed before. Maybe you've even been baptized. But the question isn't what you've done—it's Who you're trusting. Salvation is not in a prayer, baptism, good works, or church membership. Salvation is in Jesus Christ alone.

The Bible says:

- **We are all sinners.** *"For all have sinned, and come short of the glory of God."* (Romans 3:23)
- **Sin carries a penalty.** *"For the wages of sin is death…."* (Romans 6:23a) This death is not just physical but eternal separation from God in hell.
- **Jesus paid the price for our sins.** *"…but the gift of God is eternal life through Jesus Christ our Lord."* (Romans 6:23b) *"But God commendeth his love toward us, in that, while we were yet sinners, Christ died for us."* (Romans 5:8)
- **We must receive Him by faith.** *"…if thou shalt confess with thy mouth the Lord Jesus, and shalt believe in thine heart that God hath raised him from the dead, thou shalt be saved . . . For whosoever shall call upon the name of the Lord shall be saved."* (Romans 10:9, 13)

Salvation is not about fixing yourself first or bringing God an offer. It's coming to Him with nothing—empty-handed—and trusting in Christ's finished work on the cross.

Will You Trust Him Today?

If you don't know for sure that you're saved, I urge you: don't wait. Right now, you can pray from your heart something like this:

"Lord, I know I'm a sinner. I believe You died for me and rose again. I turn from my sin and place my trust in You alone as my Saviour. Please forgive me and save me. Amen."

There's nothing magical about the words—it's about truly believing and surrendering to Christ. If you will come to Him by faith, He will save you—just like He saved me.

INTRODUCTION: WHEN GOD LETS US HEAR THE ENEMY

Years ago, fresh out of business school—*when I still had hair*—I was working for a global consulting firm. I landed on one of those consulting-firm projects with all the usual ingredients: big personalities, smiles on the surface, knives under the table. In other words, it was one of those very "professional" environments where everybody smiled like they were at a wedding but strategized like they were invading Normandy.

There was a colleague on that project who was senior to me by about a year. She was smart, capable, polished, and very much at home in that dog-eat-dog environment. She was also the one assigned to train me. From the beginning, there was obvious tension. We clashed. I tried to keep things professional and avoid unnecessary friction, but the bad blood was there early.

At one point, we were working in San Francisco for the week, and I came back home to Ohio for the weekend. While I was home, she sent me an email. The email itself was fine—pleasant, polished, helpful. It sounded like she wanted to keep training me and keep things moving forward.

But below that email, in the thread she apparently didn't realize was still attached, was a completely different conversation. She had been trashing me to another colleague—not constructively, not in any measured way, but in a way clearly meant to shape the story before she went to the project manager. It was obvious she intended to say she had tried to train me and that I simply was not working out.

And just like that, I had information I was never supposed to see. I had gotten a glimpse behind the curtain. I knew what she was saying when she thought I was not listening, and I knew what she was planning before she made her play.

And that changed how I handled everything. I reached out to the manager first. I didn't retaliate. I didn't try to destroy her. In fact, I was honest about her strengths, because she did have them. I had learned from the project. I had benefited from some of her knowledge. So, I said so. And then I volunteered to take myself off that project, since there was another local opportunity with the company that made more sense. In one move, the whole thing changed. The tables turned. Her plan got spoiled because I had seen what I was not supposed to see.

Now, that coworker was not "the enemy" in the biblical sense, and I'm not making that moral comparison. But that experience has stayed with me because it illustrates something simple and useful. Sometimes a man is given a glimpse of information that changes how he understands the battle in front of him. Sometimes a man gets to hear what is being said in private, and suddenly the whole strategy becomes visible.

Scripture gives us many warnings about the devil.[1] It shows us his work, his devices, and his fingerprints all over temptation, deception, accusation, bondage, and ruin. We see unclean spirits speaking. We see devils tormenting. We see Satan resisting, tempting, filling hearts, sifting men, blinding minds, and accusing the brethren. We even have passages in Isaiah and Ezekiel that seem to pull the curtain back on the pride and downfall associated with Satan. But in terms of Satan's own recorded words, Scripture gives us only a few snapshots.

In the garden, he speaks.

In Job, he speaks.

In the wilderness, he speaks.

Genesis 3. Job 1-2. Matthew 4.[2]

That's it.

The God who wastes no words saw fit to preserve those words. The Lord who gave us His Book by design, not by

---

[1] Genesis 3 identifies the tempter as *"the serpent."* Later Scripture identifies *"that old serpent"* as *"the Devil, and Satan."* (Revelation 12:9; 20:2) Paul also connects the serpent with the deception of Eve in 2 Corinthians 11:3.

[2] The parallel passage of Matthew 4 is in Luke 4.

accident, chose to let us hear the enemy at those three moments. He didn't do that to entertain curiosity or to make us fascinated with darkness. He did it because there's an advantage when God lets His people overhear what would otherwise remain behind the curtain.

2 Corinthians 2:11 says, *"Lest Satan should get an advantage of us: for we are not ignorant of his devices."* That verse sits near the center of what I want to do in this series. The Christian is not called to be obsessed with Satan, but neither is he called to be naïve about him. We are not to drift through spiritual war half-asleep.

We have an adversary. 1 Peter 5:8 does not soften that reality. *"Be sober, be vigilant; because your adversary the devil, as a roaring lion, walketh about, seeking whom he may devour."* That's not symbolic fluff. That's a warning. Be sober. Be vigilant. Why? Because we have a real enemy. He is active. He is purposeful. He absolutely is seeking whom he may devour.

I don't know all that Satan understood in those key moments. I don't know whether he knew those words would be forever recorded in the Word of God. When you call a business these days, you may hear a cheerful recording on the other end say, "This call may be recorded for quality assurance purposes." Christ didn't stop the wilderness temptation and say, "Please be advised, this conversation will be entered into the canon of Scripture." Whether Satan knew or not is beside the point. God knew, and God chose to let us hear it.

In Genesis 3, we hear the serpent question the Word of God, contradict the warning of God, and reframe rebellion as wisdom and gain. *"Yea, hath God said…?" "Ye shall not surely die." "Ye shall be as gods."* Right out of the gate, Satan's voice is exposed as crooked, insinuating, and destructive. He doesn't begin with a pitchfork. He begins with a question mark. He doesn't first say, "Hate God." He says, in effect, "Did God really say that? Is God really that good? Is obedience really necessary? Is judgment really certain? Might there be more for you on the other side of disobedience?" That's how the war begins in human history.

In Job, the scene changes dramatically. We're no longer in Eden. We're no longer dealing with innocence in a garden. We're brought into a heavenly scene and allowed to hear Satan speak about a righteous man. And what comes out of his mouth is accusation. Suspicion. Slander. Contempt for the very possibility of sincere devotion. *"Doth Job fear God for nought?"* In other words, Job is only serving You because it pays. Take away the hedge. Strip the blessing. He will curse You to Your face.

Then in the wilderness, we hear him speak again. This time he isn't speaking to Eve in innocence or about Job in suffering. He is speaking directly to Christ. The tempter comes to the last Adam. He presses appetite. He presses presumption. He presses glory without the cross. *"Command that these stones be made bread." "Cast thyself down." "All these things will I give thee, if thou wilt fall down and worship me."* And there, in the wilderness, the enemy's methods are laid bare.

So, the goal of this three-book series is not merely to inspect the enemy or to elevate Satan—God forbid. The goal is to expose him so we can better resist him.

James 4:7 says, *"Submit yourselves therefore to God. Resist the devil, and he will flee from you."* Ephesians 6:11 says, *"Put on the whole armour of God, that ye may be able to stand against the wiles of the devil."* We do not overcome by pretending there's no enemy. We overcome by standing in Christ, clothed in truth, with our eyes wide open.

So, we are going behind enemy lines.

Book One begins where Satan's recorded words first appear—in Eden. There, we hear how the enemy first brought ruin into the human story—not with a sword, not with thunder, not with open violence, but with a voice. And from that first scene, we will see the same truth that follows him everywhere: the devil may change settings, but he doesn't change character.

Christ said of him in John 8:44, *"He was a murderer from the beginning, and abode not in the truth, because there is no truth in him. When he speaketh a lie, he speaketh of his own: for he is a liar, and the father of it."* That verse does not merely tell us that Satan sometimes lies. It tells us lying belongs to him. It's native to him. It's in his speech. It's in his nature. So, when God lets us hear him talk, we're hearing more than ancient dialogue. We're hearing the enemy's voice exposed.

And we need that because this present world is loud, because deception rarely introduces itself as deception, because accusation often feels spiritual, and because temptation is almost never presented honestly.

So, let's go to the garden with our Bibles open and our minds clear, and let's listen—not with fascination, but with sobriety; not with superstition, but with Scripture; not as men trying to toy with darkness, but as believers who intend to be, in the language of Paul, *"not ignorant of his devices."*

BOOK ONE: EDEN

The enemy's first recorded weapon is deception.

CHAPTER ONE

THE SERPENT'S VOICE

The first fall began, not with a bite, but with a voice.

Before we study the serpent's method, I want to slow the scene down and step into the garden. What follows is an imaginative reconstruction of the scene from Eve's vantage point. I'm not adding to Scripture, only trying to help us see more carefully what Scripture already shows.

Entering the Garden

I don't remember coming into being the way a child remembers the first years of life. I remember awareness. I remember fullness. I remember opening my eyes into a world already whole.

There was no blur to it. No slow gathering of sense and shape. I came into a garden already spoken into order by the voice of God. Nothing was confused. Nothing was unfinished. Every leaf was green without spot. Every stream ran clear. Every creature moved in quiet order. Everything still bore the mark of God's own *"very good."*

And the first face I saw was the face of the man.

Adam.

There was strength in him, but not the kind that threatens. There was authority in him, but not the kind that bruises. He looked at me with recognition deeper than surprise, as though something missing in him had just been answered. And in that first moment, before anything was explained, I knew this much: I was from him, and yet distinct from him, fitted to him in a way no beast of the field or fowl of the air ever could.

He spoke over me with wonder and gratitude. *"This is now bone of my bones, and flesh of my flesh…"*

There was joy in his voice, and relief, and reverence for the God who had made me and given me to him.

I learned quickly that Adam already knew this place in ways I did not. He walked through the garden not as a stranger discovering it but as one already entrusted with it. He knew the rivers, the habits of the creatures, the paths by the water, and the rhythms of the place.

The Lord God had planted this garden eastward in Eden. He had caused to grow every tree that is pleasant to the sight and good for food. Pleasant to the sight. Good for food. Those words belonged to nearly everything around us.

Beauty and provision met everywhere. There was no meanness in the garden. No death. No decay. No hunger that could not be met by the open hand of God.

Adam would tell me of the day the Lord brought the creatures before him. The cattle, the birds, the beasts, each according to its kind. He named them all. Adam saw truly. He understood. He named with discernment because the wisdom of his Maker had been stamped into him. Yet for all that parade of living wonder, no help meet for him was found.

Then the Lord made me.

There are things a woman knows without needing them explained. I knew I hadn't been made to wander alone. I knew I hadn't been made apart from order, or purpose, or the God who had formed us both. Adam and I belonged to each other beneath the Lord who had made us. We weren't our own beginning. We had come from His hand.

We were free in the garden. That was the first thing. Free. There was abundance on every side. We didn't live hemmed in by denial. We lived surrounded by permission. *"Of every tree of the garden thou mayest freely eat."* I heard that word often from Adam's mouth: freely. God hadn't placed us in a prison but in a paradise.

Then Adam told me of the one command.

In the midst of the garden stood the tree of life, and also the tree of the knowledge of good and evil. Of that tree, Adam said, the Lord had spoken plainly: *"Thou shalt not eat of it: for in the day that thou eatest thereof thou shalt surely die."*

I listened carefully when he said it. Not because I doubted him, but because the command was clear, and clarity is easy to remember when there is no storm in the mind. I knew the tree. I knew where it stood. We didn't stumble upon it by accident. It stood where it stood, known and visible. The command wasn't hidden in mist. The Lord had spoken it.

And there was no bitterness in the command. Nothing in me rose up against it. Why should it? We lacked nothing. We had the Lord, His Word, the garden, and each other. What was one tree in a world full of open-handed bounty? The prohibition didn't feel cruel. It felt holy.

Sometimes Adam and I would walk in the cool of the day and speak of the Lord's goodness. There were no wounds in those conversations, no guarded glances, no old grievances. His words came cleanly to me, and mine to him. There was no hiding then. To be naked and not ashamed is harder to explain than to remember. There was no inward twisting. No fear of being exposed. No shadow in the soul that made one want to retreat behind leaves. We were open because we were unbroken.

The garden was alive in every direction. Branches stirred under the movement of birds. Water shone in the rivers like moving glass. Creatures crossed our path without fear. Fruit hung heavy and ripe. The scent of life was everywhere. I cannot say how long we lived there before the day the serpent came, because time didn't weigh upon us as it would later. There was rhythm, but not fatigue. Morning didn't threaten us with age.

Then came the day when I stood near the tree.

I was not starving. Let that be said plainly. I was not neglected. I was not driven there by hardship. The garden still glowed with the goodness of God. The command had not changed. The Lord was no less good that day than He had been the day before.

I was simply there.

The serpent was there also.

He didn't come with the appearance of ruin. Nothing in the moment announced itself with darkness and thunder. There was no roar. No warning cry rising from the beasts. The garden didn't suddenly dim. He was subtle. That's the word I would later understand best. Subtle. Not clumsy. Not grotesque. The kind of danger that doesn't first frighten, but draws near quietly.

When he spoke, it was the shock of speech more than the tone that first arrested me. Not because the world was mute. It was not. It was alive with sound. But this wasn't the sound of creation praising by doing what it was made to do. This was speech bent another way. Personal. Directed. Meant to reach inward.

"Yea, hath God said, Ye shall not eat of every tree of the garden?"

It was a question. That's what has lingered with me most. Not a command. Not an open curse. A question. But not an innocent one. Even then, though I did not yet understand the depth of its danger, something in it changed the moment. He did not begin by saying God was false. He began by making God's Word the subject of examination.

He placed it before me as something to handle, weigh, and reconsider.

And then I answered him.

Perhaps I shouldn't have lingered. Perhaps I should have turned immediately and sought Adam. But innocence is not the same thing as tested wisdom, and I had not yet learned what a crooked voice can do.

"We may eat of the fruit of the trees of the garden," I said. *"But of the fruit of the tree which is in the midst of the garden, God hath said, Ye shall not eat of it, neither shall ye touch it, lest ye die."*

Even as I spoke, the command still stood in my own words, though not as cleanly as God had first given it. The Lord had spoken. Death was attached to disobedience. I knew what should have settled the matter: God had said.

But the serpent didn't fall silent.

He pressed further.

"Ye shall not surely die."

There it was. Direct. Bare. Clean in its rebellion. The contradiction of God, spoken into the garden as though it were wisdom. He didn't tremble. He didn't hesitate. He contradicted with ease, as if the Lord's warning were the only thing in the garden not to be trusted.

Then he gave the promise.

"For God doth know that in the day ye eat thereof, then your eyes shall be opened, and ye shall be as gods, knowing good and evil."

I looked at the tree.

Had it changed? No. It stood there as it had stood before, its fruit hanging from its branches, its place unchanged, but now heavy with meaning I had not given it before. The words of the serpent seemed to wrap themselves around what I saw. I had known the tree before, but now I saw it through his words.

It looked good for food.

It was pleasant to the eyes.

And now, through the serpent's promise, it became something more in my mind: a tree to be desired to make one wise.

That desire had not been there before. Now it spoke. Now the tree seemed to gather into itself possibility. Not just fruit, but advancement. Not just beauty, but gain. Not just a tree, but invitation.

I remember the stillness of that moment.

The garden didn't vanish. The rivers still ran. The branches still stirred. Behind me, the garden was still the garden. But within me another movement had begun. The command of God stood in one place. The word of the serpent stood in another. And for the first time, those two words did not lie side by side merely as contrast. They met in conflict.

I looked again.

The fruit was beautiful.

My hand rose slowly, with a hesitation I had never known before. The branch bent lightly beneath my fingers. The skin of the fruit was smooth in my palm.

And I took it.

The First Intrusion

That's the scene. Before sin entered by the hand, it entered by the ear.

And remember where this happened. Not in a dark alley or a corrupt city, but in the garden, where everything still bore witness to the generosity of God. There was no death, no decay, no trauma, no false religion, no brokenness to blame. The setting itself testified that God was good.

Because the marvel here is that another voice entered a world where God had already spoken. There was no need for another perspective, another authority, or another word. God had spoken. And in a world where God has spoken, every competing voice is immediately suspect.

That's true in Eden, and it's still true today.

That's why this passage matters so much. The serpent spoke just forty-six recorded words. Eve answered with forty-four. Ninety words in a perfect environment, with the goodness of God on display in every direction, and the history of the human race turned.

We have now gone behind enemy lines and heard the first intrusion. Now we must bring the intel back and study the method.

CHAPTER TWO

THE DEVIL'S METHOD IN EDEN

The enemy did not stumble into Eden. He moved with method.

Genesis 3 doesn't merely preserve what the serpent said. It shows *how* he worked. The enemy in Eden was not clumsy. He was subtle, measured, and deliberate. God introduces the serpent not first by the shock of his speech, but by the cunning of his character: *"Now the serpent was more subtil than any beast of the field which the LORD God had made…"* (Genesis 3:1)

That means there is method here, and if we mean not to be ignorant of his devices, we had better study it closely. This chapter is about that method—how the serpent entered, how he picked his moment, how he framed the issue, and how he moved from question to contradiction to promise.

Men lose wars because they underestimate the enemy. They assume the enemy is simpler than he is, the attack will be obvious, and the danger will sound dangerous. Eden destroys all of that foolishness. The first recorded voice of Satan is not shrieking madness, cartoon evil, or open absurdity. It's subtle. It's plausible. It comes wrapped in conversation.

He Came into the Garden

The first thing that ought to strike us as we begin to analyze Eden is this: the devil was not planted in that garden as part of its holy order.

God planted the garden. *"And the LORD God planted a garden eastward in Eden; and there he put the man whom he had formed."* (Genesis 2:8) God placed Adam there. God gave the command there. God blessed and provided there. But God did not place the tempter there as though temptation were part of His holy design for paradise. That would violate His own character. James settles that plainly enough: *"Let no man say when he is tempted, I am tempted of God: for God cannot be tempted with evil, neither tempteth he any man."* (James 1:13) God tests and proves faith. But God doesn't tempt with evil. He doesn't inject corruption into His goodness.

Now, we know God allows what He doesn't immediately stop. Scripture makes that plain enough. But that's different from saying God planted him in Eden as part of the garden's holy order. No. The garden was God's place. The devil had to get in.

Genesis 2:15 says, *"And the LORD God took the man, and put him into the garden of Eden to dress it and to keep it."* That word *keep* is not decorative language. Adam wasn't placed there merely to admire the scenery. He was given charge. He was to tend the garden, yes, but also to guard what God had entrusted to him. Eden wasn't a playground without responsibility. It was paradise under stewardship.

And that raises a serious question: guard it from what? At the very least, Adam's charge involved more than garden maintenance and enjoying the finest piece of real estate ever handed to a man.

And if that's true, then Genesis 3 becomes even more striking. A corrupting voice is in the garden. A rival word has entered the place where God's Word had already been spoken. However we work through all the details, that much is undeniable.

Now, we need to be careful here. Scripture doesn't give us a full transcript of how Satan got there. It doesn't narrate the mechanics of that intrusion. But it does tell us enough to establish this much: Satan is a created being. He is not God. He is not everywhere at once. He moves and acts within God's world as a creature, not as the Creator.

The serpent is introduced as a *"beast of the field which the LORD God had made…"* (Genesis 3:1) In other words, the creature itself belonged to the created order Adam already knew. He had named the animals. He knew the garden. So, the striking thing was not first the appearance of the serpent as a beast, but the presence of a corrupting voice working through something familiar. The intrusion was not mainly in the form. It was in the voice.

This is why I don't think Genesis 3 begins as a scene of obvious horror. Yes, it is striking that the serpent speaks. But the deeper marvel is that a rival voice is present in the garden in the first place. However silent the intrusion may have been, it was still an intrusion.

And the devil had reason to want in.

Where else would he rather be? Where else would the hatred of hell naturally turn? Here is the man made in God's image. Here is the woman fashioned by God's hand. Here is the first marriage. Here is the place of blessing. Of course the enemy wants the garden. Of course the one who rebelled against God wants to strike at what God has newly made.

At the very least, proximity mattered. He got close enough to observe, position himself, and make his move. The devil didn't simply stumble into paradise and blurt out his line. He came into the garden first.

And once he was in, he waited.

He Picked His Moment

That's part of what makes him so dangerous. He isn't merely evil. He's observant. He doesn't lash out blindly. He looks, studies, and waits for openings.

His goal was simple enough. He only needed them to do something other than what God had said. That's the heart of temptation. Total apostasy is not required at the beginning. Just a slight deviation will do.

Now, Genesis is careful with the order of things. God gave the command to Adam before Eve was made. *"And the LORD God commanded the man, saying, Of every tree of the garden thou mayest freely eat: But of the tree of the knowledge of good and evil, thou shalt not eat of it…"* (Genesis 2:16-17) Then later, God made Eve. That matters, because Adam received the command first, and Eve received it through the order God had established. God dealt with the man first, and the man was responsible to govern his house by what God had said. That's not incidental. God is a God of order, stewardship, and responsibility.

And that order helps explain the scene.

Eve clearly knew the command. She wasn't ignorant of it. When the serpent spoke, she answered, *"We may eat of the fruit of the trees of the garden: But of the fruit of the tree which is in the midst of the garden, God hath said, Ye shall not eat of it…"* (Genesis 3:2-3) She knew the line. However loosely she handled the command, she was not standing there in total darkness.

That makes the serpent's target revealing. He was dealing with someone who knew the command and could still be moved off of it. That's still how he works.

So, why this moment?

Eve wasn't in a fallen state when the serpent approached her. Let's not read later human weakness back into paradise. She wasn't bitter, discontented, wounded, or inwardly rebellious. None of that existed yet. There was no corruption in her nature. This wasn't the devil finding a woman on a bad day, frustrated because Adam forgot an anniversary or irritated because flies got into the "not forbidden fruit salad." This was the enemy bringing a foreign voice into an unfallen world.

And that makes his timing even more significant. He didn't need Eve to be in open distress. He needed opportunity, proximity, and an opening.

He speaks when Eve is near the tree, when the conversation is directed at her, and when Adam is not answering in the scene as recorded. Later, Adam is *"with her"* when the fruit is taken and eaten. But in the conversation itself, the spotlight is Eve and the serpent. Paul later adds, *"Adam was not deceived, but the woman being deceived was in the transgression."* (1 Timothy 2:14) That verse does not excuse Adam. It condemns him in another way. But it does show that deception is central to the encounter with Eve, and the serpent's chosen point of attack fits that issue exactly.

So yes, it's fair to say the enemy picked his moment. We don't need to claim more than the text gives. But subtlety itself implies timing, patience, and precision.

That's what the devil had in Eden. He was in the garden. He knew the command in play. He had found the woman near the tree. And now, with the moment chosen, he was ready to speak.

He Opened with a Question

Before we look at the question itself, remember what kind of scene this is. Genesis 3 doesn't read like spontaneous collapse. It reads like intrusion.[3] A foreign voice has entered where it does not belong.

That's why the first move is so revealing: the serpent opens with a question.

And the question itself isn't random. He doesn't walk up and start talking about rivers or birds or the weather in paradise. He goes straight to the command: *"Yea, hath God said, Ye shall not eat of every tree of the garden?"* (Genesis 3:1) Scripture doesn't explain exactly how. But he knew where the boundary was, and he aimed for it immediately.

That shouldn't surprise us. The devil knows the Word of God better than many church members do. He isn't ignorant of God's Word. He's an enemy of it.

The command in Eden was plain: *Do not eat.* That's often where the devil strikes—not where things are hardest to understand, but where obedience is simplest. The issue is submission.

Many men imagine they would be safer if only the commands of God were more detailed. Eden destroys that excuse. The first temptation didn't come against some deep

---

[3] And this matters for more than Eden. In glory, the deceiver is cast down finally and forever: *"And there shall in no wise enter into it any thing that defileth, neither whatsoever worketh abomination, or maketh a lie."* (Revelation 21:27) Adam failed to keep Eden. Christ will keep the everlasting city.

and difficult theological system. It came against a plain command from God in a perfect environment.

That's not a small thing. It's the first crack at moving Eve out of submission and into judgment over what God had said. God had spoken. The command was plain. *"Thou shalt not eat of it."* (Genesis 2:17) It didn't need reinterpretation. It didn't need discussion. It needed obedience.

But a question, when it comes from the wrong spirit, puts uncertainty where there was supposed to be submission. It introduces the idea that what God said is now open for reconsideration. *Did He really mean it? Is that really the point? Is the command really as settled as it sounded?*

And questions, by their nature, invite engagement. They pull the target into handling what God said as though the creature now stands over the command instead of under it. That's why dishonest questions are dangerous. They don't seek light. They seek leverage.

The serpent was not a confused student seeking clarification. He wanted the command handled as a matter for discussion instead of submission.

That's one reason Scripture warns us about the wrong kind of questions. Paul tells Timothy to avoid questions that do not produce godly edifying, and he tells Titus to avoid foolish questions (1 Timothy 1:4, 2 Timothy 2:23, Titus 3:9). The Pharisees often worked the same way with Christ. They asked questions, not because they loved truth, but because they wanted leverage (Matthew 22:15). Satan started with a question because rebellion often begins there—not first with a fist raised at heaven, but with a subtle shift in posture toward what God has said.

I can remember that happening in my own life in a very practical way.

When I was nineteen, I was at the church I grew up in. I had started getting involved after high school, and I was actually given the high and holy responsibility of teaching preschool Sunday school—which, in retrospect, was probably about right for my level of maturity at the time. They probably figured at least I couldn't wreck a flannel graph. But I loved it. I loved serving in the church I grew up in.

There was an older couple who took me under their wing, and I loved the attention. It felt good to be noticed and included. Then one evening after church, we were out getting dinner together, and the wife asked me a question. Just a question. She said, "Have you ever noticed Pastor is never at the church during the week? I think he's distracted with his family."

Now the truth is, I had never paid attention to that. Not once. It had never even crossed my mind.

But that question did something inside me.

And once it was there, I started looking. I started noticing. I started evaluating. A few weeks later, I literally drove out of my way to go by the church and see if Pastor's car was there. Think about that. Nothing had changed in reality. What changed was that a question had entered. And the question had reframed the situation for me.

That's exactly how the serpent works.

He doesn't always start by handing you a conclusion. He starts by planting a question that alters how you see the whole field. He wants the command, the authority, the person, the institution, even the goodness of God itself, all to be quietly reread on his terms.

That's what he does with Eve. The question is aimed right at the heart of interpretation: *"Yea, hath God said...?"* In other words: *Are you sure? Is that really what He meant? Is that really the best reading?* Questions like that can sound intelligent, thoughtful, even sincere. But when they come from a heart that is not trying to obey, they are not the path to light. They are the path to leverage.

That's where he starts. He wants the creature looking at the Word of God through the lens of suspicion rather than the posture of faith. Once that happens, the simplicity of obedience starts to feel primitive, and plain commands start to feel negotiable. He only needed her to be willing to reconsider what God had said. And once he had that, the next move came easily.

He Made God Seem Restrictive

Once the question had done its work, the serpent had Eve exactly where he wanted her. He didn't need her eating yet. He needed her staying—near him, near the tree, in the conversation, and fixed on the one thing God had forbidden rather than the thousand things God had freely given.

That's what the question accomplished: it held her there long enough for him to begin reframing reality. This is one of the oldest tricks in the devil's book. He takes the God who gives freely and makes Him look like a God who withholds cruelly.

That's exactly what he does in Genesis 3. God had said to Adam, *"Of every tree of the garden thou mayest freely eat."* (Genesis 2:16) *Freely eat.* God didn't begin with deprivation, but with abundance. He didn't begin with a locked door, but with an open hand.

David said, *"In thy presence is fulness of joy; at thy right hand there are pleasures for evermore."* (Psalm 16:11) James says, *"Every good gift and every perfect gift is from above, and cometh down from the Father of lights."* (James 1:17) God is not the enemy of man's good. He's the source of it!

I know this in my own home. I want to bless my children. I don't wake up in the morning wondering what fresh misery I can invent for them before breakfast. When they're walking as they should, listening, and proving trustworthy, I'm glad to give them freedom, responsibility, and blessing. And when I put guardrails in place, it isn't because I'm petty. It isn't because I enjoy saying no. It's because I love them and want what's best for them. The boundary is not the opposite of love. Very often, the boundary is the shape love takes.

The one prohibition in the garden was not a denial of goodness. It was an expression of holy goodness. It showed that man was a creature and God was God, and that freedom in Eden was not autonomy, but liberty under loving authority. In a garden full of *yes*, that one *no* gave Adam and Eve a concrete place to trust God. The fall came when a foreign voice persuaded Eve to reinterpret that trust as loss and that boundary as deprivation.

That's the very place the serpent pressed.

He takes God's *"freely"* and makes Eve stare at *"not."* He moves her attention off the field of provision and onto the fence line. He gets her studying the one restriction instead of resting in the larger abundance. And once that happens, the whole scene begins to tilt.

"Yea, hath God said, Ye shall not eat of every tree of the garden?" (Genesis 3:1)

That's not what God said. But it's close enough to work.

He doesn't need a full doctrinal denial at the beginning. Sometimes he only needs a slanted frame. He only needs to recast the whole relationship so that God looks more like a taker than a giver.[4]

He wants the soul asking questions like these: *Why would God hold that back? Why would He say no? Why does holiness feel like missing out? Why does submission feel like limitation?*

Once a man begins to look at God through the lens of deprivation, rebellion starts to feel like relief. If holiness is deprivation, then disobedience begins to feel like escape. If the command is the problem, then stepping outside it starts to look like freedom.

---

[4] There is another ditch too, and the devil is content with that one as well: if he cannot get a man to cast off God's Word in the name of freedom, he is glad to bury it under manmade restrictions in the name of righteousness. But in Eden, he is pushing the first lie. He is trying to make God look unreasonable.

Eve was deceived. She was not reaching for evil because it looked evil, but because the serpent had made it look good. The command hadn't changed. The tree hadn't changed. But the frame had changed.

And that brings us to one of the most revealing moments in the whole encounter. Once the serpent had reframed the command, Eve answered—and in answering, she exposed that the Word of God was no longer being handled with exactness.

He Worked on a Loosened Word

The serpent had a strategy before Eve ever opened her mouth. But once she answered loosely, he had exactly what he needed. He didn't need to know every detail in advance to be deadly. He only needed Eve to mishandle the Word—and she did.

God had said to Adam, *"Of every tree of the garden thou mayest freely eat: But of the tree of the knowledge of good and evil, thou shalt not eat of it: for in the day that thou eatest thereof thou shalt surely die."* (Genesis 2:16-17) That's the command. It's plain. It's exact. It includes God's liberality, boundary, and warning. Freely eat. Do not eat of that tree. Thou shalt surely die.

Now listen to Eve's response: *"We may eat of the fruit of the trees of the garden: But of the fruit of the tree which is in the midst of the garden, God hath said, Ye shall not eat of it, neither shall ye touch it, lest ye die."* (Genesis 3:2-3)

That's *not* exact. And in a war where the Word of God is the issue, exactness matters.

First, she added to the Word. *"Neither shall ye touch it."* God hadn't said that. Scripture does not record that command anywhere. Now, I'm not going to claim certainty where God has not spoken. It's possible Adam said that as a practical safeguard. It's possible Eve inferred it. It's possible she added it in the moment. But whatever the source, the point is the same: she put words in God's mouth that He had not said.

God later warned Israel, *"Ye shall not add unto the word which I command you, neither shall ye diminish ought from it…"* (Deuteronomy 4:2). Proverbs says, *"Add thou not unto his words, lest he reprove thee, and thou be found a liar."* (Proverbs 30:6) When God speaks, man does not improve the sentence. Man does not strengthen it by adding to it.

Because once Eve added *"touch,"* the serpent had a fresh angle to exploit. Once she had made the restriction bigger than God made it, the devil could work in the space between what God actually said and what Eve thought He said. And if Eve treated the added restriction as a test case—if she touched and no immediate judgment fell—the lie would only have seemed more plausible.

And Eve didn't only add. She removed too.

When God gave the command, He began with bounty: *"thou mayest freely eat."* (Genesis 2:16) But when Eve repeats the command, the *"freely"* is gone.

She says only, *"We may eat…"* (Genesis 3:2)

That may sound small to some ears, but it's not small. She trimmed off the tone of divine generosity. She quoted the rule without the warmth. She repeated the permission without the liberality. And when *"freely"* drops out, the command already feels a little colder than it really is.

Then she softens the warning too.

God had said, *"thou shalt surely die."* (Genesis 2:17) Eve says, *"lest ye die."* (Genesis 3:3)

Again, that's not exact.

"Surely die" is settled. It's direct. It's certain. *"Lest ye die"* sounds less definite. It sounds like danger has been blurred a little around the edges. The sharpness of judgment is dulled. The certainty of the sentence is softened.

In just one reply, Eve does three disastrous things. She adds where God did not speak. She removes where God did speak. She softens what God had made plain. The greatest weapon she had in that moment was the Word of God, and she handled it badly.

That's why exactness with the Word matters so much. Psalm 119 says, *"Thy word have I hid in mine heart, that I might not sin against thee."* (Psalm 119:11) Hebrews says, *"For the word of God is quick, and powerful, and sharper than any twoedged sword…"* (Hebrews 4:12) Mishandling the Word is never a harmless mistake in Scripture. It brings ruin.

Nadab and Abihu offered *"strange fire before the LORD, which he commanded them not."* (Leviticus 10:1) That's the issue right there. *"Which he commanded them not."* That's all it took. Not gross paganism. Not open atheism. Just worship altered from what God had already said. And fire went out from the Lord and devoured them.

By the time Jesus came, the Pharisees had become masters of this kind of thing. They loved the Bible on their lips and ignored it in their traditions. Christ said, *"Making the word of God of none effect through your tradition…"* (Mark 7:13) That's terrifying. A man can quote Scripture, carry Scripture, defend Scripture outwardly, and still make the Word of God of none effect by the way he handles it.

And that's a warning to every one of us. If the Word of God is our sword, don't dull it. If the Word of God is our defense, don't alter it. If the Word of God is our guide, don't add our own lines and call them His. And never trim off the parts that show His generosity, His goodness, and His plainness. Mishandle the Word, and ruin is never far behind.

Satan heard the loosened Word, and he knew exactly where to strike next.

Once the warning had been softened and the command had been mishandled, the devil moved from probing the weakness to attacking it outright.

He Denied the Warning

The serpent now says openly what he has been working toward from the beginning: *"And the serpent said unto the woman, Ye shall not surely die…"* (Genesis 3:4)

God had said, *"thou shalt surely die."* (Genesis 2:17) And once Eve had loosened that warning, the serpent stepped right into that place and flatly denied what God said.

He is not merely disagreeing with God. He is making God look untrustworthy, as though the warning were exaggerated and the danger were not real.

God warns because He is merciful. Satan denies because he is murderous.

God does not warn man because He delights in burdening him. He warns because He knows exactly where sin leads. He sees the end from the beginning.

Moses stood before Israel and put it plainly: *"See, I have set before thee this day life and good, and death and evil."* (Deuteronomy 30:15) A few verses later: *"I call heaven and earth to record this day against you, that I have set before you life and death, blessing and cursing: therefore choose life…"* (Deuteronomy 30:19) That's the heart of God. He doesn't hide the end. He doesn't mumble the consequence. He says this path leads to life, and this path leads to death. Choose life.

But the serpent always says the same thing in one form or another: *No, it does not. No, it will not. No, you will not.*

That's his game. He removes the end from view. He sells the pleasure and buries the funeral.

And once a man stops believing God about consequences, almost anything can be made to look safe.

This is why Satan loves to get men to test the edges. *Touch it. Try it. Move a little closer. See what happens. You'll find out the threat was overblown. You'll find out you can handle it.*

A man reaches for what he was told to leave alone, and because lightning doesn't strike in the first five seconds, he decides the warning must have been false.

But the delay of judgment is never the cancellation of judgment.

No, you will not surely die.

No, this will not cost you.

No, the warning does not apply to you like it applies to other people.

That's the same sermon hell has always preached.

Samson played with Delilah and kept getting away with it, until suddenly he didn't. Judges says, *"he wist not that the LORD was departed from him."* (Judges 16:20) That's one of the most terrifying sentences in Scripture. He thought the consequence would keep waiting. Then one day it didn't.

James traces the whole sequence with terrifying simplicity: *"But every man is tempted, when he is drawn away of his own lust, and enticed. Then when lust hath conceived, it bringeth forth sin: and sin, when it is finished, bringeth forth death."* (James 1:14-15) God tells you the end in advance: death. Satan says, *No, not really.* God says judgment. Satan says, *No, not like that.*

And it's not only physical death, though physical death surely entered through sin. It's also ruin working inward and outward at once: shame, fear, hiding, bondage, and separation from God. Death began to work in every part of the human story the moment God's warning was treated as negotiable. *"For the wages of sin is death…"* (Romans 6:23) Not "might be." Not "could be." *Death.*

This is why the warning of God must never be treated lightly. It's not exaggeration. It's not emotional manipulation. It's not the overreaction of a restrictive God. It's the mercy of a holy God telling the truth about a road that ends in a grave.

Because once the consequence is removed, rebellion becomes easy to market. Once the warning is dismissed, disobedience can be made to look not only safe, but wise.

He Sold the Lie as Wisdom

That's exactly where the serpent goes next. Once he denies the warning, he replaces it with a promise. It's not enough for him to say, *"Ye shall not surely die…"* (Genesis 3:4) He gives Eve a different way to read the whole situation. Satan never wants sin to look like naked rebellion. He wants it to look like insight, advancement, and wisdom. He doesn't advertise the fruit as the bite that will trade paradise for thorns, sorrow, sweat, and a cemetery for the whole human race. No, this is enlightenment. This is progress. This is surely the better deal. Bon appétit.

"For God doth know that in the day ye eat thereof, then your eyes shall be opened, and ye shall be as gods, knowing good and evil." (Genesis 3:5)

That opening word matters: *For.* He has just said, *"Ye shall not surely die"* (Genesis 3:4), and now he gives his explanation. In other words, *here is why you will not die. Here's the real story. Here's what God is not telling you.* The serpent is not merely contradicting God. He is reinterpreting reality.

He is preaching a doctrine of what lies on the other side of disobedience.

God had said, *"in the day that thou eatest thereof thou shalt surely die."* (Genesis 2:17) Satan says, *"in the day ye eat thereof, then your eyes shall be opened…"* (Genesis 3:5)

Both statements mark a threshold. God says the threshold leads to death. Satan says the threshold leads to enlightenment. God says crossing the line brings judgment. Satan says crossing the line brings awakening.

It's the same line, but God and Satan tell two completely different stories about what lies on the other side of it. The boundary hasn't changed. Only the story attached to it has changed.

"Then your eyes shall be opened…"

Again, that sounds good. Opened eyes sound like blessing. Scripture speaks that way often. *"Open thou mine eyes, that I may behold wondrous things out of thy law."* (Psalm 119:18) Sight, in the biblical sense, is good. But Satan hijacks the language of opening and detaches it from submission. He offers sight through disobedience. He offers awakening by stepping over the line God drew.

"Ye shall be as gods…" (Genesis 3:5)

Once more, that sounds elevated, noble, almost spiritual. He's making disobedience look like promotion. He's saying, in effect, *God is withholding a higher condition from you. God is keeping you from becoming more.*

The devil loves to tempt men, not only with pleasure, but with promotion. Not merely with appetite, but with elevation. He knows that many people would refuse a temptation that looks base but will run toward one that looks spiritual, intellectual, or mature. Dress rebellion in the language of growth, and many souls will call it wisdom.

And then comes the closing phrase: *"knowing good and evil."* (Genesis 3:5) At first glance, that sounds like discernment. But that's not what the serpent is offering. He isn't offering wisdom through the fear of the Lord. He is offering knowledge by trespass. Scripture is clear about where wisdom begins. *"The fear of the LORD is the beginning of wisdom…"* (Proverbs 9:10) Not flirting with evil. Not tasting evil by experience. Departing from evil. That's understanding. Godly wisdom never begins by stepping over God's Word. It begins by bowing under it.

And that word *knowing* in Genesis 3:5 should not be treated as light or casual. Scripture often uses it to speak of intimate, experiential knowledge: *"And Adam knew Eve his wife…"* (Genesis 4:1) It's one thing to know by revelation that evil is evil because God says so. It's another thing entirely to know evil by stepping into it. The serpent was offering Eve not discernment from above, but knowledge from within. Not wisdom through trust, but knowledge through transgression.[5]

That same lie is still with us. The world—and the devil behind it—says that you need to try it for yourself, cross the line to understand the line, and taste darkness to appreciate

---

[5] This pattern of category inversion appears throughout Scripture. Isaiah pronounces a woe on those who *"call evil good, and good evil"* (Isaiah 5:20), and a few verses later explains why: *"they have cast away the law of the LORD of hosts, and despised the word of the Holy One of Israel."* (Isaiah 5:24) When men stop trusting the Word, they begin redefining good and evil for themselves.

light. That's why James contrasts heavenly wisdom with another kind entirely. *"This wisdom descendeth not from above, but is earthly, sensual, devilish."* (James 3:15) There's a sight that is actually blindness. Satan was selling that kind of wisdom in Eden.

In the scene with Eve, the deception reaches its high point here: the serpent takes the very thing that brings ruin and markets it as wisdom.

He Let Appearance Preach for Him

At this point, the serpent stops talking. He has said enough. The battle came through the ear, but now it moves to the eye. Satan has finished speaking, and Eve begins seeing.

Genesis 3:6 says, *"And when the woman saw…"* There it is. That's the hinge. The lie has settled deeply enough that Eve now begins to read the tree through the serpent's lie instead of through God's Word.

That's how deception works. The suggestion gets in, and then the heart begins doing the rest. In Eden, we're watching deception begin to reshape desire in real time.

The first thing Eve sees is this: *"the tree was good for food…"* (Genesis 3:6)

In other words, it looked useful. It looked like something that could satisfy. That's what made the temptation so deceptive. Fruit isn't evil, food isn't evil, and appetite itself isn't evil. The issue was never that the tree had become filthy, grotesque, or materially corrupt. The issue was that something apparently good was now being evaluated apart from the Word of God.

That's always a dangerous shift. What seems useful is not always righteous. What appears beneficial is not always holy. Saul thought sparing the best of the animals made sense, but Samuel answered, *"to obey is better than sacrifice…"* (1 Samuel 15:22) Usefulness isn't the final test. God's Word is.

Then the text says the tree was *"pleasant to the eyes…"* (Genesis 3:6)

Now the temptation deepens. What first looked useful now looks beautiful. Scripture warns about this again and again, because the eye is not neutral. Achan said, *"when I saw among the spoils a goodly Babylonish garment… then I coveted them, and took them…"* (Joshua 7:21) David *"from the roof saw a woman washing herself; and the woman was very beautiful to look upon."* (2 Samuel 11:2) The eyes see, the heart interprets, desire rises, and the hand follows.

That's why Paul says, *"we walk by faith, not by sight."* (2 Corinthians 5:7) Sight is a poor master. The flesh gets very clever at approving what merely looks good.

And then the third layer appears: *"a tree to be desired to make one wise…"* (Genesis 3:6)

Now the temptation is no longer merely about appetite or beauty. Now it's about elevation. The tree is interpreted as a pathway upward.

That's what makes this especially deadly, because wisdom is a good thing. Scripture tells us to seek wisdom. The problem wasn't that wisdom was bad. The problem was the way she was reaching for it. Eve was reaching for wisdom apart from submission. She was no longer content to know good and evil by trusting what God said. She wanted to assess reality for herself.

And that's the heart of rebellion. Not merely, *I want the fruit,* but, *I want the right to interpret reality on my own.* The temptation wasn't simply to choose bad over good, but to take what seemed good apart from God.

That's why the word *good* in Genesis 3:6 matters so much. In Genesis 1 and 2, God is the One declaring what is good. Good is not creature preference, but God's verdict on a world functioning inside His order. But in Genesis 3, the woman now sees the tree as *"good for food"* in defiance of God's revealed Word. The fruit hadn't changed. It was likely beautiful, edible, and desirable. But God had spoken. That's the shift.

And that's still how compromise usually works. Not by a person saying, *I want wickedness because it is wicked*, but by saying, *This feels right. This seems helpful. This appears wise.* The serpent attacks the boundary, and then the soul begins calling boundary-crossing good.

This is why 1 John 2:16 shines such a floodlight back on Eden: *"For all that is in the world, the lust of the flesh, and the lust of the eyes, and the pride of life, is not of the Father, but is of the world."*

Good for food: lust of the flesh.

Pleasant to the eyes: lust of the eyes.

Desired to make one wise: pride of life.

John names the pattern. Paul warns where that pattern lands: *"lest by any means, as the serpent beguiled Eve through his subtilty, so your minds should be corrupted from the simplicity that is in Christ."* (2 Corinthians 11:3)

The battlefield is the mind. Once the tree is reread through the lie, the hand isn't far behind. Eve first received the serpent's reinterpretation. Then she reassessed the tree through it. And once the forbidden thing looked useful, beautiful, and elevating, appearance could finish the sermon by itself.

He Was Gone When Judgment Came

One of the most revealing details in the whole account is what happens after the act is done. Once the fruit was eaten, once the line had been crossed, and once the serpent had gotten what he wanted, he was gone from the scene. That's not an accident. He's there for the question, the reframing, the lie, and the false promise. He's there while the mind is being worked on, while the heart is being stirred, and while the hand is moving. But when judgment begins to fall, when shame rushes in, when fear enters, and when the sentence starts to unfold, the serpent is nowhere to be found.

Genesis 3 says, *"She took of the fruit thereof, and did eat, and gave also unto her husband with her; and he did eat."* (Genesis 3:6) Then what? The serpent doesn't step forward and comfort them. He doesn't say, "I will stand with you now." He doesn't defend them before God. He doesn't carry the weight with them. Instead, *"the eyes of them both were opened, and they knew that they were naked…"* (Genesis 3:7) Shame enters. Exposure enters. Then they sew fig leaves together. Then they hide. *"And Adam and his wife hid themselves from the presence of the LORD God amongst the trees of the garden."* (Genesis 3:8)

The serpent is gone.

And now Adam and Eve are left standing in the awful reality of what sin actually brought. Not enlightenment, liberty, or promotion, but shame, fear, hiding, and distance. That was what waited on the other side of the line. God had told the truth all along.

That's still how the devil works. Christ said of him, *"He was a murderer from the beginning…"* (John 8:44) He doesn't love the people he tempts. He doesn't cherish the souls he deceives. He's no liberator or guide. Jesus said, *"The thief cometh not, but for to steal, and to kill, and to destroy…"* (John 10:10) That's the devil's mission: to steal, to kill, and to destroy. And one of the clearest proofs of it is that he never stays around when the destruction arrives.

Hellish counsel never stays to pay the bill.

Proverbs says of the strange woman, *"Her house inclineth unto death, and her paths unto the dead."* (Proverbs 2:18) But sin never introduces itself that way. It flatters, glows, and seduces. Proverbs 7 says the young man goes after her *"as an ox goeth to the slaughter"* and *"knoweth not that it is for his life."* (Proverbs 7:22-23) Satan always works to hide the end until it's too late.

The devil got Eve looking. He got Eve wanting. He got Eve taking. He got Adam eating. And once he had done that, he was content to leave them to face the holy God whose Word he had just contradicted.

That ought to sober every one of us. One of the devil's great lies is not only that there will be no judgment, but that he will somehow still be there when it comes. But he never is. He's not a friend to sinners, but their destroyer.

And what happened next in Eden proves it. God comes into the garden. *"And the LORD God called unto Adam, and said unto him, Where art thou?"* (Genesis 3:9) The issue is now between the sinners and the God they disobeyed. Adam answers, *"I heard thy voice in the garden, and I was afraid…"* (Genesis 3:10) That's one of the saddest lines in Scripture. The voice that should have been sweet now brings fear. Fellowship is broken. Innocence is gone. The serpent had promised opened eyes, and in one sense he hadn't lied about that part. Their eyes were opened all right, but they were opened into shame.

Then the Lord pronounces judgment. The woman will have multiplied sorrow. The man will toil in a cursed ground. Death will now work in the race. *"Dust thou art, and unto dust shalt thou return."* (Genesis 3:19) And even the serpent himself is judged. *"Upon thy belly shalt thou go, and dust shalt thou eat all the days of thy life."* (Genesis 3:14) The devil is not in charge of the ending. God is. The serpent can deceive, but he cannot write the final sentence.

And right in the middle of that judgment comes the first note of victory: *"It shall bruise thy head, and thou shalt bruise his heel."* (Genesis 3:15) Even there, in the wreckage of the fall, God announces that the serpent will not have the last word. Christ will.

If chapter two has taught us anything, it's that the devil is a master of setup, but he's never lord of the outcome. He can get into the garden, pick his moment, open with a question, make God seem restrictive, loosen the Word, deny the warning, and sell the lie as wisdom. But when judgment comes, he will not save the soul he ruined, reverse the sentence, cover the shame, restore the fellowship, or fix what he broke.

Only God can do that.

It is madness to follow the voice that never pays the bill.

And if we're honest, this is still exactly how he works today. He whispers in the temptation and goes silent in the consequences. He helps people cross lines and then leaves them to sort through the rubble.

That's why this analysis matters. We have listened carefully to the enemy's first recorded words and traced the method. We now know how the serpent enters, frames, presses, lies, sells, and leaves.

That strategy hasn't changed.

CHAPTER THREE

THE PATTERN THAT STILL SPEAKS

What happened in the garden was not merely the first temptation. It was the pattern.

We have slowed the scene down and studied the serpent's method. Now, we must do something with what we've learned. Otherwise, this is just a careful study of the tripwire followed by, "Well, that was enlightening," and then KABOOM.

Intel only helps if you act on it.

So, this is the doing chapter. We're not walking back into Eden to stare at the tree. We're walking back in to learn where the tripwire is, how the pattern works, and how to interrupt it before it does its damage.

In Eden, the issue was plain: *do not eat.* The serpent's whole deception was aimed at getting Eve to cross the line God had clearly drawn. In our lives, the issue may take different forms. Sometimes it's something God forbids. Sometimes it's something God commands. Sometimes it's a truth we must hold, a restraint we must honor, a warning we must heed, or a boundary that protects obedience. But the point of this chapter is not to build a giant catalog of every possible issue. The point is to expose the tactic. The devil's goal is always the same: get a man to disobey what God has said.

And knowing that is not enough.

You see, there's no shortage of information in our day. We're drowning in content—sermons, podcasts, clips, books, debates, threads, hot takes, reels, and endless commentary. A man can know a great deal and still do very little. That's one of the great dangers of our age: we mistake being informed for being obedient.

But truth has to get shoe leather. Doctrine has to be put to work. The Christian life isn't effortless. I often tell my kids, if it's not hard, you're probably not doing it right. We're not going to walk through a cursed world, face a real devil, feel the pull of the flesh, and live in spiritual conflict without friction. Of course there will be effort. Of course there will be resistance. Of course there will be moments when you have to say no, hold your line, and refuse to reopen matters God has already settled in His Word.

And if we're going to have victory, we have to learn to recognize the devil's tactics early—not after the fruit is already in the hand, not after the damage is done, but when the first question begins working on the mind.

When the First Question Hits

Before anybody reaches for the fruit, the battle has already started. *"Yea, hath God said…"* Those are not just old words in an old garden. They're the opening move, the first pry bar under the door.

It starts with the first inward shift from certain to negotiable, from anchored to loosened, from "God said" to *Well, maybe.* In many cases, you're not out hunting for compromise. Things may be going along just fine. Then a question mark slips into your mind and reopens a matter that used to have a period on it. The serpent doesn't need to move you all at once. He just needs to crack open what God already closed.

And that can happen in all sorts of ordinary ways now. A snarky comment online. A disgruntled friend dropping a sentence in your ear. A podcast clip that flatters your frustration. A correction you didn't like. A moment you keep replaying because it hurts. Usually, the devil doesn't begin with a full-blown argument. He begins with a slant. A suggestion. A quiet, "Have you ever thought maybe…" A little sentence that lands in the flesh and stays there.

Maybe they meant that at you. Maybe that boundary is the problem. Maybe you are being controlled. Maybe you do not have to be that careful. Maybe you have been missing out. That's how the question starts to take hold—especially around convictions and the standards that protect them.[6]

But a standard that helps you obey God isn't your enemy. When a conviction is grounded in God's Word, it's not meant to train you to drift from Him. It's meant to help you stay close. And once a line is clear, that's usually where the pressure begins: to loosen it, question it, or move away from it.

Psalm 119:89 says, *"For ever, O LORD, thy word is settled in heaven."* Malachi 3:6 says, *"For I am the LORD, I change not…"* So, when God settles something, the danger isn't that He will change, but that we will. And usually that change doesn't begin with open disobedience. It begins with a question mark.

Now, there's a difference between honest questions and serpent-style questions. I'm certainly not against searching the Scriptures for understanding. That's definitely my thing. But I'm absolutely against giving audience to thoughts that are trying to loosen settled obedience. There's a world of difference between a man who goes to the Word for stronger conviction and a man who entertains a question because he wants a weaker one.

That's why James 1:8 says, *"A double minded man is unstable in all his ways."* The serpent doesn't need open

---

[6] By conviction, I mean a matter the Holy Spirit settles in a man's conscience through the Word of God. By standard, I mean a practical boundary a man adopts to help guard obedience to that settled matter. For example, if a man becomes convinced that certain entertainment feeds his flesh and pulls his heart away from Christ, that's the conviction. A standard flowing from that conviction may be that he chooses not to have streaming services so he has more control over what comes into his home through the television. The standard itself is not holiness. It's a guardrail.

compromise first. He just needs the mind to wobble. No firm ground. Just whatever voice is loudest this week.

And boy, do we have *a lot* of voices now. Everybody has a podcast, a comment section, and a sudden ministry of helping you relax where God told you to be careful. 2 Timothy 3:14 says, *"But continue thou in the things which thou hast learned and hast been assured of..."* Jude said we are to *"earnestly contend for the faith which was once delivered unto the saints."* Once delivered. Not endlessly redesigned because somebody persuasive made compromise sound mature.

So, when *"Yea, hath God said?"* hits your mind, recognize the tactic immediately. Not after it has turned into a whole system of reasoning. Not after a line has been crossed. Right there. At the first question mark. Because the danger is what happens next—when you let that thought sit there, replay it, nurse it, and start building a case for it.

Right there, ask: *Is this thought helping me obey God, or is it loosening what God has already said?* If it's doing the latter, don't entertain it. Take it straight back to Scripture and put the issue under the plain Word of God. And if Scripture has already closed the issue, shut the file before the thought has time to take hold.

The reason is simple: the serpent isn't asking because he needs information. He's asking because he wants access. That's why you cannot be careless about what you let into your mind. Some voices don't come to strengthen obedience. They come to reopen what God already settled. So, the first lesson from Eden isn't complicated, but it's urgent: guard the period God has placed where the serpent wants to insert a question mark.

When the One Who Said "No" Becomes the Villain

Once the question is allowed to linger, the next move is usually not doctrinal but relational.

At this stage, the heart is not ready to say outright, *God is wrong.* So, resentment fastens itself to whatever blocks what I want—the correction, the expectation, the command—and then to the person connected to it. The rebellion is not framed at first as *God is my problem,* but as *these people are my problem.* The pastor, the church, the parents, the husband—the people who said "no" and would not move the boundary—start looking like the issue. Sometimes that resentment fastens itself to tone, style, or personality, but underneath it is still resentment of the limit itself. Often, before the heart openly reaches for the forbidden thing, it first turns the line—and then the person attached to it—into the villain.

That's what happened in Eden. The serpent didn't begin by making the tree beautiful. He began by making the command feel restrictive. That's how deception often works. The devil doesn't start by making the wrong thing look right, but by making the right thing look unreasonable. Once that happens, disobedience hardly needs selling. He cannot get you to love destruction outright, so he gets you to resent the fence that keeps you from it.

I can remember being a little boy at my grandma's house. I had found a stray kitten outside and played with it all day. When night came, she would not let me bring it inside. And she was right. The kitten likely had fleas, and it just wasn't a good idea. But I wasn't upset about the wisdom of the rule. I was upset with Grandma. So, I did what any deeply offended little sinner might do: I went to my room, pouted, drew a picture of my grandmother as the devil, wrote "you're mean" on it, and left it on her easy chair. No, I did not literally think my grandma had horns and a pitchfork. But I did exactly what resentment does: I turned the person enforcing the rule into the villain.

And that's usually when the vocabulary changes. Now it's *control. Legalism. Cult. Conformity. They only love you if you comply.* Listen carefully to that kind of language. It often tells you what's happening in the heart. We're no longer just dealing with the command itself. The one guarding the line has now become the villain.

And let me be careful here, because authority can certainly fail. Pastors can be harsh. Husbands can be selfish. Parents can provoke. Standards can be applied with pride and hypocrisy. That's true. But that's not the same thing as saying all authority is bad. The issue is not whether authority is above scrutiny. The issue is whether the heart is taking a real failure and turning it into permission to throw off a restraint God actually gave. The flesh loves to take an exception and turn it into a theology. A person gets wounded, irritated, corrected, frustrated, or simply told no, and before long every guardrail is treated as abuse, every standard as oppression, every warning as manipulation, and every conviction as extremism. That's not discernment. That's resentment reaching for moral vocabulary—words that make rebellion sound righteous.

And once resentment has that vocabulary, everything starts getting reread through those words. Modesty becomes suppression. God-given roles become domination. Pastoral warning becomes control. What was once a guardrail is now called a cage. Then the slogans take over: "Come as you are," "Don't judge," "Unconditional love"—phrases often used to redefine love as affirmation without correction. In that world, the one who says "no" can never seem loving, while the one who removes the boundary will almost always look loving.

But that's not Bible love. Proverbs 3 says, *"My son, despise not the chastening of the LORD… For whom the LORD loveth he correcteth…"* True love *"rejoiceth not in iniquity, but rejoiceth in the truth."* (1 Corinthians 13:6) It doesn't flatter sin or bless someone's drift. It tells the truth, warns, corrects, and loves enough to oppose what destroys. In Scripture, love and restraint live in the same house. One of the devil's great lies is to sever love from authority, as though love never says no, never warns, never confronts. But that's not love. That's abandonment dressed up as kindness.

That's why Satan starts here. If he can make the warning sound cruel, the danger will start sounding attractive. If he can make the authority look oppressive, disobedience will start sounding reasonable on its own.

And there's often a false sense of relief in that moment. Once the fence is treated as the problem, stepping away from it can feel lighter. But lighter is not always safer.

The other voices don't stay neutral either. The voices that planted the question now sound helpful—even heroic. They seem to understand you. They validate what you feel. The one who warned you sounds harsh, while the one who moves the line sounds wise, compassionate, and free. And it usually doesn't stop there. You start leaning toward the voices that relieve the pressure and away from the ones that would steady you again. Once that happens, the very people who might have helped you recover start sounding like obstacles instead.

So, when the one who said "no" starts looking like the villain, stop and ask what's really happening. Has authority actually failed, or has my heart begun to resent restraint? Am I seeing this through Scripture, or through suspicion? Have I confused correction with cruelty?

Because once the warning voice starts sounding like the problem, the thing God said "no" to will not stay neutral for long. It will grow bigger, brighter, and more desirable.

When the One "No" Takes Over

In Eden, it was one "no" in a sea of "yes." But once the heart turned against the restraint, that one "no" began to swallow the whole scene. What was once one boundary among many blessings became the central thing in view. The field of vision narrowed. Gratitude faded. Proportion disappeared.

Psalm 103:2 says, *"Bless the LORD, O my soul, and forget not all his benefits."* Deception does the opposite. It makes a man forget God's benefits and fixate on the one thing God has forbidden. That one thing starts outweighing everything else. And when gratitude dies, that's often a sign that something is wrong in the way we see God.[7]

And when that happens in real life, it usually shows. A man starts replaying the restriction in his mind, and before long it starts showing up in his speech. He circles back to it in conversation more than he realizes. He talks about it with edge, irritation, cynicism, and sarcasm—with that thin layer of humor people use when they want to make a boundary look ridiculous. What was once simply a point of obedience becomes a point of agitation. The kindnesses of God begin to feel small, while the one thing denied begins to feel central. The "no" starts living rent-free in his mind.

Romans 7 helps explain what is happening here. When Paul says, *"I had not known lust, except the law had said, Thou shalt not covet,"* (Romans 7:7) he is not blaming the command. A few verses later he says the commandment is *"holy, and just, and good."* (Romans 7:12) The problem was not that God said "no," but what the sinful heart did in response to God's

---

[7] Scripture repeatedly connects gratitude to a right view of God. In Romans 1, men *"glorified him not as God, neither were thankful"* (Romans 1:21), and a false view of God quickly followed. In Colossians 3, letting *"the word of Christ dwell in you richly"* is joined with thanksgiving (Colossians 3:16-17). In Galatians 5, walking in the Spirit stands against the rule of the flesh, and throughout the New Testament a Godward, Spirit-governed life is marked by thanksgiving rather than craving. When a man stops being thankful, that is often not merely a mood problem, but a vision problem.

"no." The flesh starts acting as though the command is the issue, when the real issue is the heart that resents being denied.

And once that denial becomes the focus, the matter is no longer being weighed in the fear of God. It's being weighed under the pressure of the one consuming thought. That's a dangerous place to make decisions.

The flesh rarely introduces that thought honestly. It doesn't usually say, *I want to disobey God.* It says, *I just need peace. I just need room. I just need to be understood. I just need balance.* The flesh likes to put a suit and tie on lust and call it wisdom. That's how sinful desire starts dressing itself up as discernment.

A husband can have a faithful wife, healthy children, a roof over his head, a church, a Bible, and a thousand evidences of God's goodness, yet become mentally consumed with the one woman who is not his. The complaint is never about the ninety-nine kindnesses. It's about the one restriction.

By that point, you're no longer reading life through gratitude, but through the one thing denied. You're no longer asking, *How has God been good to me?* You're staring at the one thing He said "no" to. You're standing at the fence, staring through it at what you can't have.

You start telling yourself, *If only that one restriction were gone, then I would be free. I would be happy. Life would finally open up.*

And when a man reaches that point, he has often been making smaller compromises for a while. He lingers where he used to leave. He listens longer than he should. He revisits what he ought to have cut off. He keeps the conversation going. He starts managing the edge instead of fleeing it. Long before the fruit is taken, a man is often already walking circles around the tree.

That's what distortion does: when one denied thing fills the view, abundance starts feeling empty. Israel did this. God had delivered them out of Egypt, divided the sea, fed them from heaven, given them water from the rock, and led them by cloud and fire, yet they said, *"But now our soul is dried away: there is nothing at all, beside this manna, before our eyes."* (Numbers 11:6) *Nothing at all?* They had bread from heaven. But the thing they wanted had made abundance look small.

Proverbs 27:20 says, *"hell and destruction are never full; so the eyes of man are never satisfied."* The eyes of man do not naturally say, "Enough." They reach past lawful blessings and keep straining after what they cannot have. Once that one thing swells out of proportion, the soul stops seeing clearly.

And once the one "no" has grown that large in the mind, the words standing in the way will not stay settled for long. The command starts feeling too stiff. The wording starts feeling too plain. And when that happens, sinners do what sinners have always done: they start loosening the Word of God.

When the Word Starts Getting Loose

A man doesn't usually throw the Bible away at first. He just starts handling it differently. At this point, he's no longer coming to Scripture to be corrected, but to find relief.

That's what happened in Eden. Eve didn't deny the command. She loosened it. *"Surely die"* became *"lest ye die."* She added where God had not spoken and softened where God had been plain. It was close enough to sound spiritual, but not exact enough to guard obedience. And once the handling of the Word gets loose, the conscience loosens right along with it.

That's how it still happens today. The words may be on the page, but the force of them gets softened. The text gets qualified, explained away, buried under exceptions, or pitted against some other verse fragment until the original point no longer lands with the weight God gave it. A man doesn't usually walk up and say, *This verse is false.* He says, *That's not really what it means. You have to look at the culture. That was for that time. There are different interpretations. You're being too literal. That's your conviction, not mine.*

The verse is still there. But it's been declawed.

This is the point where a man can still sound biblical while moving steadily away from obedience. He may still quote verses. He may still talk theology. But the Bible is no longer standing over him as judge. It's being recruited as counsel for the defense.

And this is where it gets painfully practical. Spend five minutes online, and somebody will weaponize a half-verse before your coffee even cools.

A man gets bothered by correction, and suddenly *"Be ye kind one to another..."* (Ephesians 4:32) becomes his favorite verse. Never mind that the same Bible says, *"Open rebuke is better than secret love"* (Proverbs 27:5) and *"Faithful are the wounds of a friend…"* (Proverbs 27:6) Kindness gets pulled out and used like a club against correction itself.

Or a person wants to recast all restraint as unloving, so now *"God is love"* gets repeated as though that settles everything. But love is being quoted, not to understand God as He has revealed Himself, but to mute the parts of His character that are no longer convenient.

Or a man wants freedom from moral scrutiny, so now *"Judge not"* becomes a slogan. But the same Christ who warned against hypocritical judgment also said, *"Judge not according to the appearance, but judge righteous judgment."* (John 7:24) That's how the Bible gets weaponized: not bowed to, but brandished.

And once a man learns to use Scripture that way, the next move is usually predictable: he becomes very interested in the sins of everybody standing in his way.

He starts finding verses about pride, harshness, hypocrisy, bad leadership, and lack of compassion—not to tremble at Scripture, but to discredit the one who said "no." And of course, those sins are real. But finding somebody else's sin in the Bible doesn't excuse mine. A flawed messenger doesn't suddenly make my disobedience safe.

Clearly, that's not honest handling of the Word of God. It's the flesh using Bible language to justify what it already wants. And today, that kind of thinking has gotten a lot more convenient, because temptation suddenly comes with a search bar.

A man doesn't even have to wrestle in silence anymore. He can type what he wants and find a hundred ready-made voices eager to help him justify it. Not, *What does the Bible say about this?* but, *Why this may not be wrong after all.* Not, *Help me understand holiness,* but, *Why church standards are legalism.* Not, *What does Scripture teach?* but, *Why Christians are too strict about this.*

Of course support can be found when the question itself is already loaded. Once the conclusion is already chosen, the study is crooked before it even begins. If a man wants permission, he'll find someone to turn every caution into fear, every boundary into bondage, and every restraint into man-made tradition. If he wants to stay bitter toward the one who corrected him, he'll find a whole online choir ready to sing about trauma, toxicity, control, oppression, and fake love.

That's not Bible study. That's permission shopping with a concordance.

The right question, then, is not, *How do I get the Bible to permit what I already want?* The right question is, *What does the Bible actually say?* Not what helps my case. Not what flatters my frustration. Not what weakens the warning. But what does the text actually say?

All of this exposes the same problem: God has spoken, but the heart doesn't want to hear what He has said. In Luke 16, Abraham said, *"They have Moses and the prophets; let them hear them."* When the rich man protested, Abraham answered again, *"If they hear not Moses and the prophets, neither will they be persuaded, though one rose from the dead."* The issue was not a lack of information, but resistance to the Word already given. That's still the issue today. The problem isn't that the Bible is unclear. The problem is that the heart doesn't want what Scripture has already made clear.

And that's why this matters so much: when the Word gets softened, the conscience gets softened too. That's how a man gets from conviction to compromise without ever announcing that he rejected the Bible. He didn't throw it away. He started trimming where God was sharp, balancing where God was plain, adding where God was silent, and explaining away what God meant to press home.

So, we need to be brutally honest about it. If I'm only interested in verses that expose other people, but not the ones that expose me, I'm in danger. If I have patience for texts that loosen restraint, but none for texts that tighten obedience, I'm in danger. If something in me says, *I don't want that verse to mean what it appears to mean,* I'm in danger. If I'm searching for support instead of truth, relief instead of light, and permission instead of purity, I'm in danger.

When that is what I see in myself, there's only one honest move: go back to the text and let it speak plainly. Refuse the loaded question. Refuse the flattering search. Refuse the selective quotation. Ask, *What exactly does God say?* Then let it stand there in all its force, whether it confirms what you want or cuts against it.

If we will not let the Bible say what it says, we will make it say almost anything.

And once that happens, the next stage is never far behind. Once the text is loosened enough, disobedience no longer looks dangerous. It starts looking reasonable. It starts looking mature. It starts looking compassionate. It starts looking like wisdom.

And that's exactly where the serpent wants you.

When the Wrong Thing Starts Sounding Reasonable

Now the heart starts building its case.

At first, temptation feels like tension. There's still an inward fight. You know what God said, and you know what you want, and the two are colliding. But once you have adjusted the command just enough and softened the edges of what God said, the battle changes. You're no longer merely wanting the wrong thing. You're now defending it.

That's exactly what happened in Eden. What God forbade was reread as opportunity. Deception does not usually tell you to run at evil because it is evil. It teaches you to reinterpret evil until it feels reasonable.

The heart is remarkably skilled at this. Scripture says, *"There is a way which seemeth right unto a man, but the end thereof are the ways of death."* (Proverbs 14:12) Not a way that looks wicked. A way that seems right. That's the danger. It feels right. It sounds right. It arranges itself in the mind like a compelling argument. *"Every way of a man is right in his own eyes: but the LORD pondereth the hearts."* (Proverbs 21:2)

That's where many people lose the battle: when desire starts making speeches. James says that a man is *"drawn away of his own lust, and enticed."* (James 1:14) Lust doesn't merely pull. It entices. It argues.

A man usually doesn't say, *I want emotional closeness with a woman who is not my wife.* He says, *My marriage has been hard, and this person just understands me.* A believer usually doesn't say, *I want to lower the standard.* He says, *I want more grace, more balance, more nuance.* A young person usually doesn't say, *I want the world.* He says, *I just don't think everything has to be so extreme.*

That's the shift. We're no longer just staring at the tree. We're defending the tree.

Rebellion gets renamed as growth.

Compromise gets renamed as wisdom.

Worldliness gets renamed as relevance.

Disobedience gets renamed as peace.

That's why Isaiah said, *"Woe unto them that call evil good, and good evil…"* (Isaiah 5:20) Because once a man begins renaming things, he becomes very hard to reach. If darkness is now light in his mind, correction feels offensive. If bitterness is now discernment, pride is now conviction, and compromise is now wisdom, then the soul is no longer merely tempted. It's self-justifying.

At that point, the heart starts gathering evidence for its case—every disappointment, frustration, unmet desire, difficult conversation, and perceived slight—and arranges it into one clean conclusion: *therefore, this is the right move.*

That's why this stage feels so logical to the person in it. He's no longer wrestling with whether he wants it. He has moved on to explaining why he should have it.

Saul is a painful example of this. God gave a plain command through Samuel in 1 Samuel 15, and Saul disobeyed it. But when Samuel confronts him, Saul doesn't fall down and say, "I rebelled." He starts building the case. *"Yea, I have obeyed the voice of the LORD…"* (1 Samuel 15:20) Then he explains the sheep and oxen by saying the people took them *"to sacrifice unto the LORD thy God…"* (1 Samuel 15:21) Disobedience put on religious clothes. Saul didn't defend his compromise by saying, "I wanted what God forbade." He defended it by saying, "I had a better reason."

That's how sin usually works. It rarely introduces itself honestly. It doesn't say, *I will destroy you.* It says, *This is what you need right now.* Proverbs 30:20 gives the chilling summary: *"Such is the way of an adulterous woman; she eateth, and wipeth her mouth, and saith, I have done no wickedness."*

And that story usually gets more detailed as it goes. The forbidden thing begins to shine with exaggerated promise. It starts looking useful, beautiful, necessary, even wise—the missing piece that will finally make everything work. That's one of the surest signs that you're deep in deception: when one forbidden thing starts looking like salvation.

And once the case has been built, anything that interrupts it starts to feel threatening. A person may be genuinely hurt, leave a church, and need honest help. But watch what can happen next: the story goes public, the comments start helping build the case, and what began as, *This hurt me,* hardens into, *Therefore the love was fake, the standards were bondage, the leadership was control, and the whole place was rotten.* Once that public case gathers a chorus behind it, anyone who doesn't affirm it starts looking cold, blind, or dangerous. "You don't understand." "Don't judge me."

"You're being too rigid." Many times, that's not depth. It's insulation from interruption.

And once that inner argument gets strong enough, you're very close to action.

That's why this stage cannot be handled casually. If you realize you're building a case for what God has forbidden, you need interruption immediately. You need someone who loves you enough to tell the truth and loves God enough not to applaud your argument. The fence you have been resenting is not keeping you from life. It's keeping you from ruin.

Because once the heart has built a glowing case for sin, it stands at the edge of a dangerous next step.

When Judgment Starts Looking Small

This stage is about shrinking the cost.

The heart may want the thing. The mind may have built the argument. The Word may have already been softened. But before the hand moves, the conscience still feels the weight of what God said would happen.

What will this cost? What will come of this if I go forward?

So, the lie goes there next.

That's exactly what happened in Eden. God hadn't left the warning vague. He said, *"in the day that thou eatest thereof thou shalt surely die."* (Genesis 2:17) But when the serpent answered, he didn't merely say, "Eat the fruit." He went after the warning: *"Ye shall not surely die."* (Genesis 3:4)

He shrank the cost until disobedience felt survivable. He made God's warning sound exaggerated. He didn't need Eve to think there would be no consequences at all. He only needed the warning to feel less certain than God had made it.

You'll be fine.

That's still how the lie works. It doesn't have to erase the warning. It only has to make the warning feel less urgent, less certain, less serious.

The heart says, *It's not that big of a deal.*

But Galatians 6:7 says, *"Be not deceived; God is not mocked: for whatsoever a man soweth, that shall he also reap."* That verse leaves no room for negotiation. Not what a man hoped to reap. Not what he meant to sow. Not what he planned to fix before harvest time. Seed has a harvest.

The heart says, *One more time won't hurt.*

But Proverbs 6 asks, *"Can a man take fire in his bosom, and his clothes not be burned?"* The answer is obvious. Fire does what fire does. Sin does what sin does. A man can call it small, controlled, temporary, understandable, or manageable. But it's still fire. It still burns.

The heart says, *Nothing has happened yet.*

But Ecclesiastes 8:11 says, *"Because sentence against an evil work is not executed speedily, therefore the heart of the sons of men is fully set in them to do evil."* That's exactly how the heart misreads delay. Consequences don't always come instantly, so the heart begins to imagine they're not coming at all.

God's patience is not Him saying, *This doesn't matter.* It's Him giving room to repent. And when a man uses that room to go deeper into sin, he hasn't escaped judgment. He has only misunderstood the delay.

The heart says, *I can get right with God later.*

That's not repentance. That's presumption. It's not a broken man running back to mercy. It's the flesh trying to make mercy part of the plan. God is merciful, but His mercy is not permission to schedule rebellion. Grace isn't a way to get what I want now and clean it up later.

That's the lie: I can have the sin and keep the peace. I can cross the line and control the damage. I can step into disobedience now and get right with God on my own terms.

Romans 6:1-2 cuts through that bargain: *"What shall we say then? Shall we continue in sin, that grace may abound? God forbid."* Grace does not make sin safe.

The heart says, *Nobody will know.*

But Numbers 32:23 says it with frightening simplicity: *"be sure your sin will find you out."*

Not maybe. Not perhaps. *Be sure.*

That doesn't always mean public exposure in the exact form we imagine. Sin may find a man out in his marriage, in his mind, in his children, in his ministry, or in his spiritual deadness. But it will find him out.

The heart says, *This only affects me.*

But David proves otherwise.

In the moment, everything probably looked containable. A private look. A private inquiry. A private encounter. A private cover-up. A private arrangement.

But it wasn't private before God, and it didn't stay private in its effects. Nathan said, *"Now therefore the sword shall never depart from thine house."* (2 Samuel 12:10) Then he said, *"by this deed thou hast given great occasion to the enemies of the LORD to blaspheme."* (2 Samuel 12:14)

David's sin touched his house, his testimony, his usefulness, the enemies of God, and the name of God in the eyes of others.

So no, it does not only affect you. Sin reaches farther than the moment, the room, or the person who commits it. And above all of that, it is against God.

That is what David finally saw when he said, *"Against thee, thee only, have I sinned, and done this evil in thy sight."* (Psalm 51:4) He wasn't denying that he had sinned against Bathsheba, Uriah, his household, and the nation. He was showing where the deepest offense really was.

And that is the real issue underneath this whole stage. Judgment starts looking small because God starts looking small.

Psalm 36:1 says, *"The transgression of the wicked saith within my heart, that there is no fear of God before his eyes."* That's the diagnosis. Not merely poor judgment. Not merely a rough season. Not merely emotional exhaustion.

No fear of God before his eyes.

A man begins looking at sin as though heaven is not watching, God will not act, and holiness is only a sermon word.

But Isaiah 66:2 gives the opposite posture: *"to this man will I look, even to him that is poor and of a contrite spirit, and trembleth at my word."*

That's what has been lost. Trembling.

Not editing the Word. Not relabeling sin. Not negotiating consequences. Trembling at what God has said.

And let me be clear. This does not mean a saved man loses his salvation every time he sins. But it does mean sin is no small matter for a saved man. The Father who keeps His children also chastens them. If you belong to Him, you are not free to sin safely.

Sin will not unsave the child of God, but it can break communion, choke usefulness, deaden spiritual hunger, damage your home, and leave death behind it.

That's where this stage leaves a man. Sin sounds reasonable, and judgment sounds distant. The warning that once stopped him now feels exaggerated. The line he once feared crossing now feels manageable. He begins treating God's mercy like permission, God's patience like approval, and God's silence like absence.

Once a man has built the case for sin and shrunk the warning attached to it, the next step is painfully close.

The fruit is already in the hand.

When the Story Becomes the Fruit

One mistake we can make is reading Genesis 3 too narrowly. We picture the forbidden fruit as only the bottle, the website, the text thread, the affair, the lie, the theft—the thing a man can point to and say, "There. That's the forbidden fruit."

Sometimes the fruit is obvious. But not always. Sometimes what a man takes is not something he takes into his hand, but something he takes into his heart: a version of events that flatters self, feeds hurt, hardens suspicion, and makes distance, division, or disobedience feel reasonable.

In those moments, the temptation is not first, *I want to do something wicked.* It's, *I think I finally see this clearly now.*

That's what makes it so dangerous. It doesn't feel like rebellion. It feels like discernment. But real discernment is willing to be tested by Scripture; suspicion only looks for evidence to justify the verdict it has already reached.

That's closer to Eden than we often realize. Before Eve reached for the fruit, the serpent gave her a different story about God, His command, the tree, herself, and the consequences. Once that story got inside her, the act was not far behind.

That still happens. A look, a silence, a delayed reply, or an awkward sentence can become the seed of a whole case. Sometimes the enemy doesn't tempt a man first with adultery, drunkenness, or theft. Sometimes he tempts him with a story—a suspicion he cannot prove, an offense he keeps rehearsing, a way of reading the situation that makes him feel wounded, righteous, and justified. A man can carry on a private war with someone who doesn't even know he's on the battlefield.

That's why this matters so much in churches, marriages, families, friendships, and ministries. Many people have never touched the obvious "fruit," but they have fed on suspicion for days. They have nursed offense in the dark. They have taken one awkward interaction and let it outweigh years of faithfulness. They have used isolated verses, not to search their own heart, but to prosecute someone else.

"He that answereth a matter before he heareth it, it is folly and shame unto him." (Proverbs 18:13) *"He that is first in his own cause seemeth just; but his neighbour cometh and searcheth him."* (Proverbs 18:17) That's not a small issue. That is not harmless. That is another voice doing work in the soul.

And notice how closely it follows the same Eden progression. The question enters: *Why did he say that? Why did she do that? Why did that feel so cold?* Then the person becomes the villain. One perceived slight fills the horizon. The good gets forgotten. Charity weakens. Scripture gets edited—not to search the heart, but to build the case. Bitterness gets renamed as discernment. Distance gets renamed as wisdom. A harsh spirit gets renamed as conviction. And before long, cynicism, disunity, estrangement, and a poisoned heart no longer feel serious. The story feels too important to question.

Many people have fed deeply on that story without ever calling it temptation.

They call it "being honest." They call it "finally seeing things clearly." They call it "using discernment." They call it "just putting some pieces together." But if those pieces were put together in the flesh, under suspicion, without prayer, without humility, without the facts, and without charity, then a man is not feeding on truth. He is feeding on a story that is doing the serpent's work.

To be clear, this does not mean every concern is imaginary. Sometimes there really is a problem. Sometimes a person really was sharp, careless, unkind, or wrong. Sometimes something truly does need to be addressed. But even when something real is in front of us, the flesh can still turn it into something larger, darker, and more self-serving than it actually is. Satan does not need a completely fictional event. He is often content to take something small, real, or ambiguous and build a fortress around it.

That is where *"charity...thinketh no evil"* becomes more than a sweet phrase. It becomes protection. And that is where the warning about a *"root of bitterness"* becomes painfully practical, because bitterness does not stay contained. It springs up and troubles more than the person who first nursed it (1 Corinthians 13:5; Hebrews 12:15).

So, widen the warning. This chapter does not only apply when the forbidden thing is scandalous, visible, and easy to name. Sometimes the battle is quieter than that. Sometimes it happens in the private courtroom of the mind, where the thing you are tempted to take is a version of events that makes you feel injured, important, and right.

Once a man starts feeding on that, he can get very far from God while still looking outwardly restrained.

That's why it must be recognized early—before the story settles in, before suspicion hardens, before the case gets built, before prayer disappears, before bitterness starts dressing itself up in the language of wisdom.

By the time a man is withdrawing, dividing, confronting in the flesh, or walking away, the real battle has usually been going on for quite some time.

He didn't start with his feet.

He started with the story he believed.

That's Eden too. And if Eden teaches us how the pattern works, it also teaches us where the pattern can be broken.

How to Break the Pattern

By the time Eve took the fruit, the battle had already been decided upstream. You don't wait until the hand touches the fruit to fight. You fight earlier—at the ear, in the imagination, and in the heart. *"Keep thy heart with all diligence; for out of it are the issues of life."* (Proverbs 4:23)

So, how do we break the pattern?

First, end the conversation early. The serpent had no authority over Eve. He was dangerous because he was given audience. The moment another voice begins to reinterpret what God has plainly said, the safest move is not dialogue. It's refusal. Don't "hear it out." Don't let it pace around in your mind as though it has a right to be there. The first question mark is already dangerous. The longer that conversation continues, the more danger there is that what was once settled will start to feel negotiable.

Second, return to the light. Eve had no business continuing a private exchange with the serpent as though that voice deserved the floor. Deception grows in isolation. One of the first practical steps in any temptation is to get out of your own thoughts and back into the light, where the lie is no longer the only voice in the room. Private deception is not beaten by private thinking. *"He that trusteth in his own heart is a fool…"* (Proverbs 28:26) God gave pastors, parents, a church, and faithful friends—not only to comfort us when life is hard, but to help rescue us when our own hearts start telling us a dangerous story.

And if that story has turned a person into the villain, go talk to that person with a humble spirit when it is safe and appropriate to do so. Not with folded arms. Not with a prepared speech. Not like a prosecutor walking into court. Go as a Christian who knows his own heart can lie to him. Many times, the person you have turned into the enemy is one of the very people God could use to interrupt the deception. That's why the story must be dragged into the light. Proverbs 18:17 says, *"He that is first in his own cause seemeth just; but his neighbour cometh and searcheth him."* A private case can sound airtight until another godly voice searches it.

Third, go back to what God actually said. Not the serpent's paraphrase. Not your own softened version of the command. God's voice. If you want to stay out of the tree, you must stay close to the Book. You must know God's words well enough that a strange voice sounds strange. When the serpent starts paraphrasing reality, something in you should immediately say, *That is not what God said. That is not what God is like. That is not where that path goes.* The safest Christian is not the one with the strongest personality. It's the one who stays nearest to God's Word.

Fourth, get away from the tree. There comes a point in temptation where distance is wisdom. The Bible does not teach us to negotiate with temptation. It teaches us to flee. *"Abstain from all appearance of evil."* (1 Thessalonians 5:22)

"Flee also youthful lusts." (2 Timothy 2:22) *"Make not provision for the flesh, to fulfil the lusts thereof."* (Romans 13:14) That's strong language because temptation often requires strong action. Many people want peace while still leaving the door unlocked. They want purity while still protecting the pipeline that supplies the impurity. But if something is feeding the appetite, the fantasy, the resentment, or the compromise, cut it off. Leave the tree before the tree fills the whole field of vision.

While the story is loud, do not make major decisions. Do not leave the church, end the relationship, send the message, make the announcement, change the standard, or move the boundary while your heart is raw and your mind is full of accusation.[8] The pressure to act immediately is often part of the deception. Slow down long enough for Scripture, prayer, and godly counsel to test the story.

Fifth, remember the garden. God did not place Adam and Eve in a barren field with one forbidden tree in the middle. He placed them in a garden and said, *"Of every tree of the garden thou mayest freely eat."* Deception shrinks the garden and magnifies the boundary. So deliberately count the mercies. God's commands are not theft. They are protection. Maturity is not seeing how close you can get to the edge without falling. It is learning to love the fence because you trust the One who built it.

---

[8] This is not counsel to remain in danger, tolerate abuse, conceal criminal behavior, or delay seeking protection when protection is needed. It is counsel not to let a heated, untested story make decisions that should be made under Scripture, prayer, truth, and wise counsel

Finally, recover the warning. God had not been vague. *"Thou shalt surely die"* was not an overstatement. It was mercy in the form of warning. *"By the fear of the LORD men depart from evil."* (Proverbs 16:6) The fear of God restores proportion. It reminds us that no private sin is private, no compromise is small, and no act of disobedience is detached from His holy sight. When the warning starts shrinking in your mind, drag it back to full size. Remember where this path goes. And above all, remember that sin is evil because God is holy.

That's how the pattern gets interrupted before the fruit is taken.

But what if the hand has already moved? What if the fruit is already eaten? What if the story has already been believed and the damage has already begun?

Then don't keep hiding in the trees.

That is where many people lose years—not only in the sin itself, but in the hiding after it. Eden does not only show us how temptation works. It also shows us what sinners do once they fall. They sew fig leaves. They hide among the trees. They shift blame. They manage appearances. They become more concerned with covering than confessing.

But hiding is not repentance. Managing optics is not repentance. Explaining yourself is not repentance. Blaming the serpent, the pressure, the season, or the people around you is not repentance.

The way back is confession.

"He that covereth his sins shall not prosper: but whoso confesseth and forsaketh them shall have mercy." (Proverbs 28:13) God does

not say mercy belongs to the man who covers best. Mercy belongs to the man who confesses and forsakes. Not confesses and manages it. Not confesses and explains it. Confesses and forsakes.

So, if you have fallen, don't sit in some fake nobility of despair. Don't act as though your only option now is to stay ruined. Run to God quickly and honestly. Run to Him with no defense brief, no polished case, and no excuse. Say what David finally said: *"I acknowledge my transgressions."* (Psalm 51:3) Run to Him, because there is cleansing there. *"If we confess our sins, he is faithful and just to forgive us our sins, and to cleanse us from all unrighteousness."* (1 John 1:9)

That's not permission to sin. It's hope for the sinner who stops hiding.

Leaving Eden with Our Eyes Open

We now know the enemy's method in Eden. He didn't begin with a bite. He began with a voice. He didn't begin by making evil look grotesque. He began by making it look good. He didn't begin by erasing consequence. He began by making judgment sound distant and manageable.

That's the pattern.

And if we can recognize the pattern, we can fight much earlier than we used to. We don't have to wait until the fruit is in the hand. We can stop at the question. We can refuse the false story. We can run from the tree. We can return to the Word. We can drag the hidden thing into the light before it becomes ruin.

But Eden also teaches us something else. The battle is deeper than behavior. A man can lose the war long before anyone sees the movement of his hand. The heart may already have shifted. The voice may already have been welcomed. The story may already have been believed.

So, we do not leave Eden guessing. We leave it with our eyes open.

The enemy is real. His method is subtle. His aim is still disobedience. And the voice that talks a man toward sin will never carry the consequences for him. The safest place is under the plain voice of God.

Before we leave this study, one more practical question needs to be answered: what should we do when someone we love is the one being deceived?

CHAPTER FOUR

WHEN SOMEONE YOU LOVE IS BEING DECEIVED

When the serpent's voice reaches someone you love, the goal is not to win the argument, but to help recover the soul.

There's one more side of deception that needs to be addressed.

It's one thing to study the serpent's words in Eden. It's another thing to watch someone you love get caught in a story that is not true. A spouse, a child, a friend, a church member, a coworker, or someone you deeply care about may begin to interpret warning as attack, love as control, caution as manipulation, and concern as hostility.

And what if, painfully, you're the villain in their story?

That's what makes deception so difficult. Once deception takes hold, everything is reinterpreted through that story. If you speak, you're controlling. If you stay silent, you're cold. If you explain, you're manipulating. If you apologize, you're managing the situation. If you bring Scripture, you're weaponizing the Bible. If you involve someone else, you're recruiting allies.

Deception does not merely distort facts. It distorts the meaning of everything around the facts. The person caught in deception rarely believes he is deceived. He believes he finally sees clearly.

So, this is not usually as simple as saying, "Hey Bob, you're being deceived."

And then Bob says, "Oh, okay. Thank you. I had not considered that. I see it so clearly now."

That would be nice.

But that's just not how this works.

So how do we help someone we believe is caught in deception without being pulled into the deception ourselves?

The answer is not one simple sentence or one perfect confrontation. We must guard our own hearts, make right what is ours, refuse to strive, speak truth with meekness, act within the role God has given us, and trust God to do what only He can do.

When Their Deception Starts Pulling on You

That begins with recognizing a danger in ourselves: deception can spread into us too. One false story in someone else's mind can start reshaping your world, your emotions, your reactions, and even the story you begin telling yourself.

The deceived person believes something untrue about you, and now you're tempted to believe something untrue in response. You're hurt because they think you hurt them. You're grieved because they are grieving over something that is not true, or not true in the way they believe. You try to explain, make peace, or bring light, but each effort is misread as another move by the villain.

You're now tempted toward bitterness, despair, and the thought, "What's the use?" You're tempted to rehearse the injustice until your own heart becomes dark. You're tempted to let the injury define you until their deception begins producing deception in you.

Elijah shows how weariness can narrow a faithful man's view. After Mount Carmel, he said, *"I, even I only, am left"* (1 Kings 19:10), though God still had seven thousand in Israel who had not bowed to Baal. Elijah was not believing Baal's doctrine, but his exhaustion had begun to tell him a false story: "I am alone. I am done. It is useless."

The false story outside of us can start creating a false story inside of us.

But there's another danger too. Sometimes the person who has been made the villain in someone else's false story doesn't become bitter or despairing. Instead, he becomes worn down by the pressure. And when he's worn down long enough, compromise can begin to look like wisdom.

This is especially dangerous for people in roles of responsibility. A pastor, parent, husband, or leader may face repeated resistance from people who misread him, accuse him, question his motives, or treat biblical boundaries as personal attacks. At first, he stands where Scripture requires him to stand. But over time, the pressure begins to work on him.

He starts to wonder, "Maybe I am being too strict. Maybe I need to loosen this. Maybe the standard is the problem. Maybe if I stop saying this so clearly, there will be more peace."

But not every accusation means we were wrong. Sometimes people are hurt because we handled truth poorly, and we'll need to deal with that honestly. But other times, people are angry because the truth is pressing on something they don't want to surrender.

So, we have to be honest both ways. We must not use "I'm standing for truth" to excuse our sin. But we also must not use "maybe I hurt them" to excuse compromise.

Saul shows us this danger. When Samuel confronted him, Saul admitted, *"I feared the people, and obeyed their voice."* (1 Samuel 15:24) He didn't say he misunderstood. He said he feared people more than he obeyed God.

That's why Paul warned Timothy: *"Preach the word; be instant in season, out of season; reprove, rebuke, exhort with all longsuffering and doctrine. For the time will come when they will not endure sound doctrine; but after their own lusts shall they heap to themselves teachers, having itching ears; And they shall turn away their ears from the truth, and shall be turned unto fables."* (2 Timothy 4:2-4)

Paul didn't tell Timothy to adjust the message every time people stopped enduring sound doctrine. He told him to preach the Word, reprove, rebuke, exhort, and do it with longsuffering and doctrine.

That's the balance: not harshness, not pride, not stubbornness for stubbornness' sake, but also not compromise because resistance has become painful.

When someone else is deceived, you must not let their deception write your story too.

Do not let their accusation make you bitter. Do not let their resistance make you harsh. Do not let their tears make you surrender truth. Do not let their anger make you afraid to obey God. Do not let their false narrative become the lens through which you see everyone else.

The Servant of the Lord Must Not Strive

Once this warning is clear, we can turn to one of the clearest passages in Scripture on helping someone caught in deception. Paul wrote to Timothy: *"But foolish and unlearned questions avoid, knowing that they do gender strifes. And the servant of the Lord must not strive; but be gentle unto all men, apt to teach, patient, In meekness instructing those that oppose themselves; if God peradventure will give them repentance to the acknowledging of the truth; And that they may recover themselves out of the snare of the devil, who are taken captive by him at his will."* (2 Timothy 2:23-26)

This passage is not merely about handling a difficult conversation. It's about helping someone who has been spiritually entangled.

Paul says they *"oppose themselves."* They think they are defending themselves, but they are actually working against themselves. They think they are free, but Paul says they are in *"the snare of the devil."*

That means the issue is not merely information. It's captivity.

That matters because we often think if we can just say the right sentence, give the right explanation, or prove the right point, the whole thing will break open. But Paul doesn't present it that way. He tells Timothy how the helper must behave, how to speak, how to instruct, how to wait, and then he says, *"if God peradventure will give them repentance."* In other words, we can speak truth, but we cannot open blind eyes. God must bring them to *"the acknowledging of the truth."*

So, the first thing this passage does is humble us.

The person caught in the snare needs truth. But he also needs something only God can give. That means our responsibility is real, but it's limited. We're not called to be passive, but we're also not called to play the Holy Spirit.

Paul begins by telling Timothy what to avoid: *"But foolish and unlearned questions avoid, knowing that they do gender strifes."*

That's especially significant after studying Eden. In Eden, the serpent used a question to create suspicion about

God's word. Not every question is wrong, but some questions are designed to generate strife rather than seek truth.

Paul says those kinds of questions must be avoided because they *"gender strifes."* They give birth to strife. They do not untangle the snare. They tighten it. Sometimes the wisest thing you can do is refuse the argument that will only feed the deception.

Then Paul says: *"And the servant of the Lord must not strive…"*

That's *not* a suggestion. Paul says he *"must not strive."*

The goal is not to win the argument, have the last word, or force the deceived person to admit you are right. The goal is recovery.

And striving almost always feeds deception.

If the person has already cast you as the villain, your intensity may confirm their suspicion. Your volume may become evidence. Your frustration may become exhibit A. Even your accurate points may be rejected because of the spirit in which they are delivered.

That does not mean truth should be watered down. It means truth must be carried in the right spirit.

Paul continues: *"…but be gentle unto all men, apt to teach, patient…"*

Gentleness is not weakness. It is not cowardice. It is not pretending nothing is wrong. Paul was no coward, yet he tells Timothy that gentleness is required.

That's hard when the deceived person is saying painful things. It's hard when he is misreading your motives, repeating a false story, or treating help like harm. But if Paul says the servant of the Lord must be gentle, then gentleness is not optional.

Then Paul says *"apt to teach."*

That means the answer to deception is not personality, pressure, or force of will. The one helping must be ready to bring the matter back to truth. And for the Christian, that means bringing it back to the Word of God. If someone is caught in a lie, the remedy is truth. Truth from God's Word, rightly used, biblically applied, and humbly delivered.

Then Paul says *"patient."*

That may be the hardest word in the entire passage.

Patience means you are not assuming this will be fixed in one conversation. You are not demanding that the person recover on your timetable. You are not measuring God's work by whether they admit it by Friday.

The prodigal son eventually *"came to himself"* (Luke 15:17), but only after the road had done its work. That's painful when the deceived person is someone you love. You want to spare them the pigpen, shorten the road, and make them see.

But you cannot make someone come to himself.

You can pray. You can speak truth when God gives opportunity. You can keep your own spirit right. You can refuse to enable sin. You can maintain necessary boundaries. You can guard what God has made you responsible to guard. But you cannot repent for someone else.

Then Paul says: *"In meekness instructing those that oppose themselves…"*

Because they are opposing themselves, meekness matters.

Meekness is not the absence of strength. It's strength under God's control. It's the ability to say more, prove more, expose more, and still hold back because the goal is not self-vindication.

If you attack the deception in the wrong way, you may strengthen it. If you come in swinging, the person may retreat further into the story. If you treat him like a fool for believing the lie, he may cling to the lie even harder. If you make the whole thing about proving yourself right, you may become part of the fog.

Truth still matters. Sin still needs to be named. Lies still need to be exposed. But the spirit must be meekness because the person is not merely misinformed. He is opposing himself.

Then Paul reminds us where our confidence must rest: *"...if God peradventure will give them repentance to the acknowledging of the truth; And that they may recover themselves out of the snare of the devil, who are taken captive by him at his will."*

God must give repentance. The person must come to the acknowledging of the truth. Then he must recover himself out of the snare.

That word *"recover"* is important. A snare is not always escaped cleanly. A person may see one thing clearly while still defending another. He may take one step toward truth and then get caught again on pride, fear, shame, embarrassment, or the consequences of what he has already done.

That's why this passage is so practical. It tells us what to avoid, how to speak, how to wait, and where to place our confidence.

Search Yourself First

But before we start applying this passage to the deceived person, we have to let it search us first.

Matthew 7 has to be taken seriously. Jesus said: *"And why beholdest thou the mote that is in thy brother's eye, but considerest not the beam that is in thine own eye? Or how wilt thou say to thy brother, Let me pull out the mote out of thine eye; and, behold, a beam is in thine own eye? Thou hypocrite, first cast out the beam out of thine own eye; and then shalt thou see clearly to cast out the mote out of thy brother's eye."* (Matthew 7:3-5)

That passage doesn't say your brother has no mote. It doesn't say there is nothing wrong with him. It doesn't say you're never allowed to help him.

It says you cannot see clearly to help him while you are refusing to deal with what is in your own eye.

So, if there's any truth at all to what they are saying, deal with that first.

Maybe you really were harsh. Maybe you spoke carelessly. Maybe you ignored them, failed to listen, overreacted, or created confusion. Maybe you really did something wrong, even if the story they built around it is not accurate.

If so, don't hide behind the word deception.

That would be dangerous.

A husband should not call his wife deceived to avoid admitting selfishness, coldness, or anger. A wife should not call her husband deceived to avoid admitting disrespect or bitterness. A pastor should not call a church member deceived to excuse harshness. A parent should not call a child deceived to avoid admitting failure to shepherd well.

Sometimes the other person is deceived, and you still sinned.

Both can be true.

So, if there is something to make right, make it right.

Be specific. Be honest. Be biblical. And please, do not apologize as a tactic. Don't confess just to regain control of the narrative. Don't say, "I'm sorry, but…" and then use the apology as a platform to prosecute the other person.

There may be a time to address the deception, but often the first step is simply to clean up your own mess and leave it there.

The temptation is to say, "I was wrong for this, but you need to understand that you are wrong about these other five things."

And maybe they are wrong about those five things.

But if someone is already reading you through a false story, your "but" may be heard as proof that the apology was not sincere. The deception may grab your explanation and use it as fresh evidence.

Sometimes the most powerful thing you can do after a genuine confession is remain silent for a while. That does not mean silence in the face of danger, abuse, or ongoing harm. It means you stop using words to control what only God can correct.

There is *"a time to keep silence, and a time to speak."* (Ecclesiastes 3:7) If you have honestly made right what you can make right, you may need to stop talking and simply pray.

Let the Holy Spirit do what your words cannot do.

And that does not mean you are passive. Prayer is not passive. Waiting on God is not passive. Refusing to strive is not passive. It may be one of the hardest acts of faith in the whole situation.

Know What God Has Made You Responsible For

But once we have made right what is ours, the question is not finished. We still have to ask what obedience requires from us in the role God has given.

Not every person in a situation has the same role. A friend, parent, husband, wife, pastor, church member, and coworker may each have different responsibilities before God.

That brings us back to Eden.

Adam was not merely a third party watching Eve struggle with a bad idea. God had put him in the garden *"to dress it and to keep it."* (Genesis 2:15) When the serpent's voice entered the garden, Adam's duty did not disappear. If anything, the danger made his duty more urgent.

The presence of deception does not remove the responsibility God has already given. A wrong voice in the garden did not cancel Adam's duty to keep the garden. In the same way, a deceiving voice in a home, church, or child's life may require the person responsible before God to act.

But this is where we need to make a careful distinction. The deceived person and the deceiving voice may not require the same response.

Toward the deceived person, 2 Timothy 2 must govern our spirit. We must not strive. The person is not the enemy. The goal is still recovery.

But toward the deceiving voice or influence, there may need to be decisive resistance. A father may need to remove an influence from his home. A pastor may need to stop false doctrine from spreading. A husband may need to say, "That influence cannot be allowed to disciple our home."

That's not striving; that's stewardship. There's a difference between attacking the person and guarding the gate.

This becomes very practical when the voice is not a snake in a garden, but a screen in a hand. The voice may be a friend, a relationship, entertainment, music, a podcast, a teacher, a social media feed, or a private message thread. The thing itself may not always be evil, but it can become a channel through which deception feeds the heart.

So first, identify the real danger. The question is not merely, "What is this thing?" The question is, "What is this thing producing in the heart?"

Is this voice producing bitterness, lust, rebellion, suspicion, false doctrine, secrecy, disrespect, neglect, worldliness, or distance from God-given authority and accountability?

Jesus said: *"Wherefore by their fruits ye shall know them."* (Matthew 7:20) If the fruit is corrupt, the voice should not be treated as harmless.

Then ask what authority God has actually given you.

If you're a parent dealing with a child, you may have direct authority to remove the device, stop the friendship, change the environment, or set a rule. If you're a pastor dealing with the church, you may have a duty to stop false teaching from spreading. Paul told the Ephesian elders to take heed to themselves and to all the flock, *"over the which the Holy Ghost hath made you overseers."* (Acts 20:28) He warned that men would arise, *"speaking perverse things, to draw away disciples after them,"* and then said, *"Therefore watch."* (Acts 20:30-31) And of certain false teachers, Paul said plainly that their *"mouths must be stopped."* (Titus 1:11) That's decisive language. There are times when a shepherd must protect the flock from a voice.

But the same principle must be applied within the boundaries of the role God actually gave. A friend should not assume the authority of a spouse. A church member should not assume the authority of a pastor. A spouse should not seize authority God has not given, and no one should use a God-given role as permission to sin. A parent may have authority, but not the right to provoke a child to wrath.

Role matters, but role does not excuse the flesh.

The point is not that everyone has the same authority. They do not. The point is that everyone has some responsibility before God.

So, before you act, ask two questions.

First, what has God made me responsible for?

Second, what kind of action does that responsibility require?

If God has given you a gate to keep, you may need to guard the gate. If God has not given you that gate to keep, you must be careful not to seize authority that is not yours. But in either case, you can pray, speak truth, refuse sin, seek wisdom, and act in the fear of God.

Speak With Wisdom, Then Trust God

Scripture gives us several patterns for wise speech. Nathan confronted David with a story before saying, *"Thou art the man."* (2 Samuel 12:7) Abigail appealed to David's future and helped him see the grief waiting at the end of his anger (1 Samuel 25). Aquila and Priscilla corrected Apollos privately instead of humiliating him publicly (Acts 18:26). Paul confronted Peter publicly because Peter's sin had created public damage (Galatians 2).

So, wisdom asks: What kind of situation is this? Is this private error, public damage, incomplete understanding, urgent danger, or an ongoing pattern that requires Matthew 18? Am I the right voice, or might this person hear another wise and spiritual voice more clearly?

James 1:5 says, *"If any of you lack wisdom, let him ask of God, that giveth to all men liberally, and upbraideth not; and it shall be given him."*

You'll need wisdom to know when to speak, when to be silent, when to apologize, when to instruct, when to involve help, when to wait, and when to act decisively.

At the same time, there are moments when others may need to be involved. Jesus gave a process in Matthew 18 for dealing with a brother who sins. The goal isn't embarrassment. The goal is to gain the brother. Proverbs 11:14 says, *"Where no counsel is, the people fall: but in the multitude of counsellors there is safety."*

But there's a difference between seeking wise counsel and recruiting allies. One is biblical humility. The other is just another version of the flesh.

This is especially important if you're the person who has been made the villain. Sometimes the deceived person cannot hear the truth from you at first. That's hard to accept. We want to be the one to fix it. We want to say the sentence that opens their eyes. But if they have already decided you are the problem, your voice may not be the first voice they can hear.

That does not mean you stop loving them. It means you humble yourself enough to admit that God may use someone else.

But if God gives you an opportunity to speak, do not waste it by merely attacking the conclusion. Ask questions that help expose the story underneath it.

God did that in Eden. After Adam sinned, God asked, *"Where art thou?"* Then He asked, *"Who told thee that thou wast naked?"* and *"Hast thou eaten of the tree, whereof I commanded thee that thou shouldest not eat?"* (Genesis 3:9, 11) Those questions exposed location, source, and action. That's still a helpful pattern.

A deceived person may need to be asked, gently and wisely: What has God clearly said? Who has had your ear? What fruit is this producing? Where does this path lead? Is this story making it hard for you to fairly hear the people trying to help you?

So, what do we actually do when we believe someone we love is being deceived?

We pray for wisdom. We search ourselves and make right what is ours. We ask what God has made us responsible for. We distinguish between the person and the voice. We act within our role. We speak truth in the right spirit. We trust God with the outcome.

The goal isn't to win the argument, but to recover the person. Truth still matters, but so does the way truth is carried. Courage still matters, but so do meekness, patience, and prayer.

Do not panic. Do not strive. Do not surrender truth. Do not feed the false story. Walk in the Spirit. Stay in the Scriptures. Tell the truth with meekness. Make right what is yours. Guard what God has given you to guard. And leave with God what only God can do.

In Eden, the enemy worked by deception.

Now we need to watch that same deception in modern clothes. The next section contains three fictional case files—not to add to Scripture, but to help us recognize the same old voice when it shows up in familiar rooms.

CASE FILES

THREE MODERN EDENS

Fictional case studies of how the pattern still speaks.

Years ago, when I was in business school at Case Western Reserve University, case studies were a major part of how we learned. You would take a real-life business situation, study the facts, analyze the decision points, and ask, *What happened here? What should have been done? Where did this thing turn?*

One of the case studies I remember was about the Tylenol crisis of 1982.

Seven people in the Chicago area died after taking Extra-Strength Tylenol capsules that had been laced with cyanide. The poison was not the result of Johnson & Johnson's manufacturing process. The best understanding was that someone had tampered with bottles after they were already on store shelves.

In other words, Tylenol itself had not created the danger. But the danger was real.

So, Johnson & Johnson acted decisively. They pulled Tylenol from shelves nationwide. Millions of bottles. Over $100 million in product. They warned the public, changed the packaging, and helped establish a new standard for consumer safety.

They treated the crisis like a crisis.

And that's the point.

Sometimes the right response looks extreme to people who do not understand the danger. But when the danger is real, decisive action is wisdom.

And if this book has shown us anything, it's that deception is real. The serpent doesn't play games. He doesn't enter the garden casually. He comes to ruin. He comes to destroy. He comes to move the soul one step at a time away from the plain voice of God.

And the terrible thing about deception is this: a deceived man usually doesn't know he is being deceived.

That's why the response has to be serious. Not dramatic for the sake of drama. Not reckless. But serious. Biblical. Immediate. Obedient.

So, before we leave Eden, I want to place three modern case files on the table.

The stories that follow are fictional composite pictures. The names are invented. The details are invented. But the patterns are not.

These things happen.

They happen in churches. They happen in homes. They happen in marriages. They happen in workplaces. They happen in the private courtroom of a man's own mind.

So, I want you to read these stories openly.

Not suspiciously toward others. Openly before God.

Don't read them thinking, *I know someone who needs this.* That may be true, but it is rarely the safest first response. Read them asking, *Lord, is there anything here that sounds like me? Is there any place where I have let the serpent's pattern begin to work? Is there any story I have been feeding? Any authority I have been recasting as the villain? Any warning I have been shrinking? Any forbidden thing I have started calling reasonable?*

And if something catches in you, don't brush it away.

That little catch may be mercy. When that happens, go back to Chapter Three. That chapter gives the way out before the fruit is taken and the way back if the fruit has already been eaten. And if one of these stories makes you think of someone you love, go back to Chapter Four before you speak. That chapter gives the spirit in which truth must be carried.

This is not the time to say, *Well, I'm sure it's nothing.* This is the time for Johnson & Johnson-style action. Recall the product. Pull it from the shelf. Deal with the danger before more damage is done.

The first case study deals with what we called in Chapter Three, "When the Story Becomes the Fruit." Sometimes the fruit is not an object. Sometimes it is a private interpretation—a version of events that flatters hurt, feeds suspicion, and makes a man feel righteous while his heart grows dark.

The second case study deals with authority, roles, standards, and restraint. One of the easiest ways to escape restraint is to rename it. Conviction becomes extremism. Standards become control. Pastoral warning becomes manipulation. Biblical correction gets labeled as abuse.

The third case study deals with marriage and adultery, or at least the road that leads there. Satan rarely begins by saying, "Destroy your home." He usually begins with the next permission. One conversation. One message. One complaint. One comparison. One secret.

So, as you read these stories, do not comfort yourself too quickly by saying, *I would never go that far.* That may be exactly the kind of confidence that keeps a man from fighting early. The better question is not, *Would I ever end there?* The better question is, *Have I already taken a step in that direction?*

Because the pattern begins upstream.

The devil doesn't mess around.

Neither should we.

Case File One: Nothing Was Ever Said

By Thursday afternoon, Daniel had already replayed the meeting twelve times.

Not the whole meeting. Just one part of it. The part where Neal praised Austin.

That was what stuck.

The team had been gathered in the conference room for the weekly project update. Same room. Same stale coffee. Same half-working speakerphone that made everyone sound like they were calling from the bottom of a well.

Daniel had come prepared. More than prepared. He had stayed late twice that week cleaning up the client presentation, fixing numbers Austin had missed, rewriting three sections, and catching an issue that would have been embarrassing if it had made it to the client.

Nobody knew that part.

Or at least, nobody had said they knew.

Neal, his manager, clicked through the slides, asked a few questions, nodded a few times, and then near the end said, "Austin, nice work pulling this together. The deck is in a much better place."

Austin smiled. "Thanks," he said.

That was it. One sentence.

But Daniel felt it land.

Nice work pulling this together.

He looked down at his notebook and circled nothing. The meeting moved on. People closed laptops. Chairs scraped against the carpet. The room emptied.

Nothing dramatic happened. No one accused Daniel. No one insulted him. No one said he was lazy, replaceable, or irrelevant.

But something had entered.

A question.

Does he even know how much I did?

By itself, that question might have been harmless. Maybe even reasonable. A man can notice something without sinning. He can feel the sting of being overlooked without building a house there. But Daniel did not let the question pass through.

He gave it a chair.

By the time he got back to his desk, the question had changed shape. *Does he even know how much I did?* became *Does he even care how much I did?*

He opened his email and tried to work, but the meeting kept replaying. Neal's voice. Austin's smile. The way nobody corrected it. The way the whole room let the sentence stand there as if Austin had carried the thing himself. Daniel clicked into the deck and stared at slide fourteen.

His slide. His fix. His late night. Austin's praise.

By lunch, he was not irritated anymore.

He was clear.

That was the dangerous part.

He did not feel like a man making assumptions. He felt like a man finally seeing a pattern. This was not the first time, he told himself. There had been the client call two months ago when Neal had thanked "the team" even though Daniel had done most of the prep. There had been the annual review where Neal said he was "reliable," which now sounded less like praise and more like a polite way of saying invisible. There had been the time Neal invited Austin and Priya into a strategy session but not him. At the time, Daniel had assumed it was because their workstreams were more relevant.

Now he was not so sure.

Now everything had a new color.

That is what a story does once it gets in. It does not merely explain one moment. It goes backward and rewrites old ones.

By three o'clock, Daniel had built a timeline: the missed praise, the strategy meeting, the lukewarm review, the "reliable" comment, the email where Neal copied Austin first, even the time Neal laughed harder at Austin's joke than his.

That last one was ridiculous, and somewhere deep down Daniel knew it.

But he kept it anyway.

A private case does not usually reject weak evidence. It uses whatever is available.

At 4:17, Neal sent him an email.

Subject: Friday deck

Daniel, can you tighten the financial assumptions section before tomorrow morning? A few parts still feel soft. Thanks.

That was all. No "great work." No "I appreciate the extra effort." No "I know you've been carrying a lot this week." Just tighten the financial assumptions. A few parts still feel soft. Daniel stared at that word: soft.

He had rewritten that section twice. He almost typed back immediately, then stopped. Not because his heart was right, but because he knew enough workplace etiquette not to put his first draft into writing.

His first draft would have been a problem.

Instead, he stood up and walked to the break room. Austin was there, leaning against the counter, scrolling his phone.

"Hey," Austin said. "Good meeting, huh?"

Daniel gave a small laugh. "Apparently."

Austin looked up. "What's that mean?"

"Nothing."

But it was not nothing, and Daniel wanted him to know it was not nothing. That is a particular kind of dishonesty: saying "nothing" with enough tone to make sure everyone knows there is something.

Austin waited.

Daniel shook his head like a man trying to be mature under great burden. "It's just interesting who gets credit around here."

Austin blinked. "What?"

Daniel shrugged. "Forget it."

But of course he did not want Austin to forget it.

Austin did not.

"Are you talking about the deck?"

Daniel looked at him. "I'm just saying, some of us worked pretty late getting that thing into shape."

Austin's expression changed. Not anger exactly. More surprise.

"Yeah," he said slowly. "I know. I appreciate it."

Daniel heard the words, but they did not fit the story, so he did not let them in.

"Sure," he said.

Austin stood there awkwardly, and Daniel walked out.

By the time Daniel reached his desk, Austin had become part of the problem. Not the main villain. Neal was still the main villain. But Austin was now benefiting from the system. Maybe knowingly. Maybe not. Either way, he was not innocent in Daniel's mind anymore.

That night, Daniel told his wife.

Not everything. Just enough.

That is usually how these stories are first shared. Not as full accusations. As fragments. As hints. As carefully arranged evidence.

"I'm just getting tired of how things work there," he said, dropping his keys on the counter.

His wife, Emily, was helping one of the kids with spelling words at the kitchen table.

"What happened?"

"Nothing new."

She looked up, and Daniel took that as permission.

"We had this meeting today, and Neal basically praised Austin for a deck I spent half the week fixing."

Emily frowned. "Did Neal know you fixed it?"

Daniel paused.

That was an inconvenient question.

"He should have."

"But did he?"

"He's the manager."

Emily nodded slowly, not fully agreeing, not disagreeing either. "I'm just asking."

Daniel felt the irritation shift toward her. That was how fast the story protected itself.

"I know. I'm not saying you're wrong. I'm just tired of always being the guy who does the work while somebody else gets the pat on the back."

Emily said, "That would be frustrating."

It should have helped.

But Daniel wanted more than sympathy. He wanted confirmation. He wanted her to say Neal was wrong, Austin was selfish, the company was blind, and Daniel was noble.

Instead, Emily said, "Maybe you should talk to Neal."

Daniel almost laughed. "That would go well."

"You don't know that."

"I know enough."

He did not, actually.

But the story had started speaking with the confidence of knowledge.

Friday morning, Daniel tightened the financial assumptions section. He did a good job. That almost made him angrier.

There is a strange bitterness that comes when a man keeps doing right outwardly while feeding resentment inwardly. The work gets done, but the soul curdles.

At 9:12, he sent the updated deck to Neal. Neal replied twenty minutes later.

This is much stronger. Thank you.

Daniel stared at the email.

In a healthier frame of mind, he might have received that as appreciation.

Daniel read it as bare minimum.

No exclamation point. No acknowledgment of the late nights. No apology for the meeting. No copying leadership to make sure everyone knew who had fixed the deck.

Just thank you.

The one "no" had taken over. Not a literal no. Not a forbidden tree in the middle of a garden. But one withheld thing: recognition. Credit. Appreciation. The sentence he wanted and did not get.

And once that one thing swelled in his mind, everything else shrank. The paycheck shrank. The steady job shrank. The decent benefits shrank. The flexibility Neal had given him when his son was sick last month shrank. The time Austin covered for him during vacation shrank. The fact that his coworkers generally liked him shrank.

All of it faded behind the one thing denied.

He wanted to be seen.

And now the lack of being seen became the center of the garden.

By Friday afternoon, Daniel was not just irritated with Neal. He was diagnosing him.

He plays favorites. He likes Austin because Austin flatters him. He keeps me in the background because he knows I'll do the work. He doesn't want me growing too much because then he'll have to deal with me.

The thoughts came easily. Too easily.

Daniel did not have proof for most of them. But proof is not always required once suspicion becomes satisfying.

On Monday, he had lunch with Nate from another department. Nate was easy to talk to because Nate enjoyed a complaint the way some people enjoy dessert. He never started with the strongest accusation. He just opened the door and let you walk in.

"You seem done," Nate said, sitting across from Daniel with a sandwich.

Daniel smiled. "That obvious?"

"A little."

Daniel leaned back. "I'm just starting to understand how things work here."

Nate nodded slowly, as though this were wisdom. "With Neal?"

Daniel did not answer quickly.

That made the answer louder.

Nate smirked. "Yeah. I've heard things."

There it was.

Another voice.

Daniel should have stopped there. He should have asked, "What do you mean?" carefully, factually, charitably. Better yet, he should have refused to feed on secondhand impressions.

Instead, he leaned in.

"What kinds of things?"

Nate shrugged. "Just that he has his people."

His people.

Daniel felt the phrase settle into him like a key turning in a lock.

That explained it.

Austin was one of Neal's people.

Daniel was not.

By the end of lunch, Daniel had more material than he had come with. Not facts exactly. Material. Tone. Impression. Hints. A few stories Nate had "heard," none of them firsthand, all of them useful.

When Daniel got back to his desk, he felt worse and better. Worse because the world now looked darker. Better because his story had witnesses.

That afternoon, he barely worked. Not because he was lazy. He would have hated that accusation. He was simply distracted by the injustice of it all. He refreshed LinkedIn twice, looked at job postings, read a thread about toxic managers, saved three listings, closed them, and opened them again.

One of the jobs was two hours away. Another was out of state. Daniel clicked through them longer than he meant to. At first, it was just curiosity. Then it became a possibility. Then, without admitting it, it became escape.

He imagined leaving. New company. New people. A place where someone would finally value him. And if that meant moving, then maybe it meant moving. Maybe they would need a new church. Maybe his responsibilities there could be handed off. Maybe Emily would see it once he explained it the right way. Maybe the kids would adjust. Maybe this was just the cost of refusing to stay where he was not valued.

He did not say it that way, of course. He called it wisdom. He called it providing for his family. He called it refusing to stay in a toxic place. He called it stewardship.

But the story was reaching for more than his job.

It was reaching for his roots.

One post caught his attention:

Never stay where you are tolerated instead of valued.

Daniel read it six times.

It felt profound.

It was vague enough to apply to anything, which made it very useful.

He almost reposted it. Instead, he copied it and sent it to Nate.

Nate replied:

Exactly.

That word did more for Daniel than he had allowed Scripture to do all week.

Because Daniel was not really going to Scripture.

Not honestly.

He still read in the mornings. A few verses. Quick. Dutiful. Enough to say he had done it. But the Bible was no longer judging the story. The story was judging everything else.

When he read, *"And whatsoever ye do, do it heartily, as to the Lord, and not unto men,"* he thought about how poorly Neal managed people. When he read, *"Let no corrupt communication proceed out of your mouth,"* he thought about how corporate culture encouraged fake positivity. When he read, *"Servants, obey in all things your masters,"* he thought, *That's not the same today.* When he read, *"Only by pride cometh contention,"* he skipped past it so quickly it barely had time to breathe.

The Word had not disappeared.

It had become selective.

That is often how it works. A man does not throw the Bible away. He just stops letting it interrupt the part of him that most needs to be interrupted.

By Wednesday, Daniel's work had changed. Not enough for anyone to accuse him of anything obvious. He was too smart for that. But enough.

Emails got shorter. Meetings got colder. He stopped volunteering extra information unless asked directly. He let Austin stumble through a question he could have helped him answer. He waited two hours to respond to Neal even though he had the answer in five minutes.

He called it boundaries.

Maybe some boundaries were needed.

But this was not wisdom.

This was punishment with professional language.

Friday brought the next moment. Neal asked him to join a quick client prep call at 4:30. Daniel saw the invitation and laughed under his breath.

Of course. Last-minute. No respect for my time.

He accepted the invite but entered the call with his camera off.

Neal said, "Daniel, glad you could jump on."

He almost said something sharp. He muted himself instead.

The call was not unreasonable. It was not even long. Twenty-three minutes. The client had changed a request, and Neal needed Daniel's help because he understood the numbers best.

In another frame of mind, he might have received that as trust.

In this frame of mind, he received it as use.

After the call, Neal stayed on.

"Daniel, do you have two minutes?"

His stomach tightened.

"Sure."

Neal's face softened a little. "I just wanted to check in. You've seemed frustrated this week. Is everything okay?"

There it was.

A door.

A merciful one.

Daniel could have told the truth. Not perfectly. Not dramatically. Just truth.

I felt overlooked in the meeting last week.

He could have said that. He could have asked whether Neal knew how much work he had done. He could have brought the story into the light while it was still young enough to be corrected.

Instead, he said, "Everything's fine."

Neal paused. "You sure?"

"Yep. Just busy."

Neal looked unconvinced but did not press. "Okay. I appreciate your work on this project. I know it's been a heavy lift."

There it was.

The sentence he wanted.

Not exactly. Not publicly. Not in the way he had imagined. But close. And because it did not come according to his script, he barely received it.

"Thanks," he said.

He left the call, then told himself Neal had only said it because he knew Daniel was upset.

That is how a story protects itself even from kindness.

By the next week, Daniel had become two people. Outwardly, he was professional, competent, present. Inwardly, he was prosecuting.

Every email had subtext. Every meeting had politics. Every compliment given to someone else was evidence. Every assignment given to him was exploitation. Every correction was disrespect. Every silence was proof.

He was not working in an office anymore.

He was living inside a courtroom.

And in that courtroom, Neal was always guilty.

Then came the client presentation. It went well. Very well. The client liked the deck. Leadership was pleased. Neal sent a note to the whole team afterward.

Great work today, everyone. Austin, Priya, Daniel— excellent job getting this across the finish line.

There was his name. Right there. Included.

But Daniel stared at the order.

Austin, Priya, Daniel.

Last.

He was last.

A month earlier, he would never have noticed.

Now it meant something.

By the time he got home that night, his heart was foul. The kids were loud. Emily asked whether he could take out the trash. The dishwasher needed to be emptied. Someone had spilled cereal under the table and apparently declared it part of the flooring.

Daniel snapped at his son for leaving shoes in the hallway.

The boy's face fell.

Emily looked at Daniel. "Hey," she said quietly. "What's going on with you?"

"Nothing."

"No. Not nothing."

Daniel exhaled hard. "I'm tired."

"I know. But you're not just tired."

He wanted to argue.

Then she said, "Is this still about work?"

That irritated him because it was accurate.

He sat down at the table. Emily sat across from him.

"Can I say something?" she asked.

"That usually means you're going to."

She ignored that.

"I think you may be building a whole story on things you don't actually know."

The sentence landed almost exactly where he did not want it.

He leaned back. "Really?"

"I'm not saying you weren't overlooked. I'm not saying Neal handled everything right. I'm not saying Austin deserved the credit. I'm saying you've been living in this for days, and I'm not sure you've actually talked to anyone who could answer it."

"I talked to Nate."

Emily's face changed.

"That's not what I meant."

Daniel looked away.

She continued, gently but firmly. "What exactly did Neal say?"

He started to answer.

Then stopped.

What exactly did Neal say?

Not what had Neal meant. Not what Daniel had inferred. Not what Nate had confirmed. Not what the LinkedIn post seemed to confirm.

What exactly had Neal said?

He had praised Austin. He had asked Daniel to tighten a section. He had thanked him. He had said he appreciated his work. He had included his name in the team email. He had asked if he was okay.

The room got very quiet.

Daniel did not like where the facts were going.

"But it's the pattern," he said, weaker now.

"Maybe," Emily said. "But maybe you made the pattern before you had the facts."

That sentence stayed with him.

Later that night, Daniel sat alone in the living room after everyone had gone to bed. The house was finally quiet. He opened his laptop, then closed it. Opened his phone, then set it down.

For the first time in nearly two weeks, the story did not feel airtight.

It felt assembled.

That was the word that came to him.

Assembled.

Built out of pieces. Some real. Some assumed. Some borrowed. Some supplied by Nate. Some supplied by his own pride.

Pride.

He hated that word.

But there it was.

He wanted recognition. That was not necessarily wicked. Work should be seen. Leaders should give credit. Injustice was real. Overlooked people existed. But something had happened inside him that was not righteous. He had not merely wanted clarity.

He had wanted to be the wronged man.

There is a strange satisfaction in that role. It gives the heart permission to be cold while feeling morally superior. It lets a man withdraw love and call it wisdom. It lets him punish people with silence while telling himself he is simply protecting himself.

Daniel saw it.

Not fully.

But enough.

He thought of Austin in the break room. He thought of Nate at lunch. He thought of Neal asking if he was okay. He thought of the job listing two hours away. He thought of the out-of-state position he had imagined somehow explaining to Emily as "what was best for the family."

He thought of his church. His Sunday school class. The people he had prayed with. The younger men he had encouraged. The place where his children were learning to serve.

And then he thought of his son's face in the hallway.

The story had not stayed at work.

Stories never do.

It had followed him home. It had made him shorter with Emily, harder on the children, colder in prayer, duller in Scripture, and less present in the very place where God had called him to lead first.

That was when it frightened him. Not because he had quit his job, announced a move, or walked away from church. He had not.

But he could see the road now.

He could see how a man gets there one justified step at a time.

First, he feels overlooked. Then he feels mistreated. Then he feels confirmed. Then he feels trapped. Then he feels wise for withdrawing. Then he feels noble for leaving. And by the time he has uprooted things God never told him to uproot, he has a whole speech prepared about stewardship, health, leadership, boundaries, and toxic environments.

Maybe sometimes those words are true.

But sometimes they are fig leaves.

Daniel knelt by the couch.

At first, his prayer was stiff.

"Lord, if I'm wrong…"

Then he stopped.

That was not confession.

That was negotiation.

He tried again.

"Lord, I have been proud."

The words scraped on the way out.

"I have been proud. I have been angry. I have assumed things I didn't know. I have enjoyed feeling wronged. I have talked when I should have been quiet, and stayed quiet when I should have talked."

By morning, Daniel knew what he needed to do.

He did not want to do it.

That was one reason he knew it was probably right.

He asked Neal if he had time to talk, and Neal invited him into his office at ten. Daniel sat down, feeling like a man voluntarily walking into surgery.

Neal smiled. "What's up?"

Daniel took a breath. "I need to clear something up. And I need to say it carefully, because I don't think I've handled it well."

Neal's expression grew serious. "Okay."

"I felt overlooked in the meeting last week when Austin was praised for the deck. I had put a lot of work into it, and I let that bother me more than I admitted."

Neal closed his eyes briefly.

"Oh, Daniel."

That was not the reaction he expected.

Neal turned slightly toward him. "I'm sorry. I should have been more specific in that meeting. I knew you had done a lot of the cleanup. Austin had pulled the first version together, and I was thinking of the overall process, but I should have recognized your work clearly. That's on me."

The apology disarmed him.

He had prepared for defensiveness.

Not this.

Neal continued, "And honestly, I've been meaning to talk to you. I've been relying on you heavily because I trust your work. But I can see how that may have felt like I was just giving you problems to fix without acknowledging it."

Daniel felt something inside him loosen. Not because Neal had been perfect. He had not. But because Neal was a person again.

Not a villain.

A person.

Daniel looked down. "I appreciate you saying that. I also need to say I let it turn into something bigger in my mind. I got cold. I assumed motives. I probably wasn't fair to you."

Neal nodded slowly. "Thank you for telling me."

There was more conversation after that. Some of it was helpful. Some of it was awkward. They talked about clearer ownership on projects, better credit in meetings, and Daniel's desire to grow. Neal was more receptive than Daniel expected.

Not everything was fixed. The habits did not disappear in an afternoon. But the story had been dragged into the light. And in the light, it looked much smaller.

Later that day, Daniel found Austin and apologized for the break room comment. Austin looked surprised.

"Thanks. I didn't really know what to do with that."

Then he added, "For what it's worth, I knew you did a ton on the deck. I should have said something too."

All week, Austin had been a character in Daniel's story. Now he was a coworker again.

By the time Daniel drove home, the office had not transformed. Neal was still imperfect. Austin still got on his nerves sometimes. Nate was still probably not the safest lunch companion. Work still had politics, pressures, blind spots, and human failure.

But the fog had lifted.

Or at least enough of it had lifted for Daniel to see the road again.

That night, after the kids were in bed, Emily asked, "How did it go?"

Daniel sat beside her on the couch.

"Painful."

She smiled slightly. "That good?"

"Probably."

He told her what happened. When he finished, he was quiet for a while.

Then he said, "The weird thing is, I really thought I was seeing it clearly."

Emily nodded. "I know."

"No, I mean it. I didn't feel deceived. I felt like I finally understood."

"That's usually how it works, isn't it?"

Daniel leaned back and looked toward the dark kitchen.

Yes.

That was exactly how it worked.

He had not eaten forbidden fruit in a way anyone would recognize from the outside. No theft. No explosion. No scandal.

He had eaten a story.

A version of events that made him feel mistreated, important, justified, and wise.

And the story had fed him. It fed his pride, his resentment, his coldness, his distance from Scripture, and his suspicion of people who had not actually become his enemies. It fed the thought that maybe he needed a new job, a new place, a new church, a new circle, a new life where nobody could make him feel overlooked again.

That was what frightened him most afterward.

How little it had taken.

One sentence in a meeting. One missing compliment. One email without warmth. One coworker willing to confirm what he already wanted to believe. One social media quote vague enough to sound prophetic. One private courtroom where Daniel got to be prosecutor, witness, judge, and victim all at once.

Nothing had really been said.

Not the thing he thought had been said. Not the thing he had reacted to. Not the thing he had carried home, fed for days, and nearly let poison his work, his marriage, his fatherhood, his church life, and his spirit.

And Daniel began to see that the goal had never been only to make him resent Neal.

The serpent had not needed a dramatic sin.

Only a question.

Does he even care?

And once Daniel let that question preach, the rest came easily. The boss became the villain. The missed recognition became the tree. The story became wise. The warning became small. The next permission became harmless.

A cold reply. A private complaint. A little gossip. A little distance. A job search. A fantasy of leaving. A dulling of Scripture. A weakening of the very roots God had given him.

Just the next permission.

And for a while, Daniel had called it discernment.

That may have been the most dangerous part.

Case File Two: The Fence Became the Problem

Lance did not think of himself as rebellious.[9]

That would have sounded too ugly. Too obvious. Rebellion was for the kid who stormed out of the house, threw his Bible in the back seat, and announced he was

---

[9] A word of caution before this case file: the point of Lance's story is not that every question is rebellion. Honest questions should be answered from Scripture with patience. The issue in this case is not that Lance has questions; it is that he begins using questions as a pathway to permission, distance, and resentment. That distinction matters.

done with church. Lance was not that. He still went to church. He still carried his Bible. He still knew the songs, the schedule, the order of service, the inside jokes, the phrases, the rhythm of it all. He had grown up there—Sunday school, junior church, youth activities, camp, bus routes, workdays, missions conference, revival meetings. His whole life had been wrapped around that church.

And for a long time, he had loved it. Or at least he thought he had.

But now he was twenty-one, living in an apartment with two other guys, working full time, taking a few classes online, paying his own bills, and finally standing outside the daily authority of his parents' house. That part felt good. Not sinful-good. Not at first. Just adult. Open. Like breathing with more room in his chest.

No one was asking where he was going every time he grabbed his keys. No one was checking what time he got home. No one was reminding him what music should or should not be playing in the car. No one was saying, "You're not wearing that to church, are you?" No one was walking past his room and noticing what was on his screen.

Freedom had a sound to it. At first, it sounded like silence. Then, little by little, it started sounding like a question.

Why did everything have to be such a big deal?

The question did not arrive dramatically. It did not kick the door down. It came in small, almost reasonable. It came one Saturday afternoon while Lance was driving home from work, listening to a song a coworker had recommended. It was not filthy. Not angry. Not the kind of thing he would have once called wicked. It was emotional, polished, well-produced, and honestly, it felt good after a long shift.

He knew the church would not approve of it. That was the first thought. The second thought came quickly after it.

Why not?

He turned the volume up. Not a lot. Just a little.

The next day, Pastor Graham preached on separation. Lance sat three rows from the back, Bible open on his lap, and felt irritation rise before the introduction was over. He had heard this before. That was what he told himself. Not, *I need this.* Not, *Is there truth here?* Just, *I've heard this before.*

The sermon was not harsh. Pastor Graham was not screaming. He read verses, explained them, gave warnings, spoke about holiness, and said that Christians should not see how close they can get to the world while still claiming to love God. A year earlier, Lance would have nodded. Now he noticed everything else. The tie Pastor Graham wore looked old-fashioned. The phrase "worldly music" sounded lazy to him. The illustration about guardrails felt childish. The warning about compromise felt exaggerated.

At one point Pastor Graham said, "A standard is not holiness, but it can protect holiness."

Lance almost rolled his eyes. Almost. He did not, because he still had enough training to know how to look respectful in church while resisting everything being said.

That is a dangerous skill.

After the service, Pastor Graham stopped him near the hallway. "Good to see you, Lance. How are things going?"

"Good," Lance said. "Busy."

"Your mom said work has been a lot."

"Yeah. It's fine."

Pastor Graham smiled. "You still praying about helping with teen conference next month?"

Lance had been. Sort of. He wanted to help. He liked being useful. He liked working with teenagers, liked being looked up to, liked feeling as though he had something to offer beyond sitting in the pew and nodding like a good church kid.

"Yeah," Lance said. "I'd like to."

"Good. Let's talk this week. I'd want to make sure we're on the same page about a few things before putting you in that role."

There it was. *A few things.* Lance felt his face stay neutral, but inside, something stiffened.

"What things?" he asked.

Pastor Graham's tone stayed kind. "Nothing complicated. Just making sure your testimony is clear, your music is right, your faithfulness is steady, and you're still walking with the Lord. You know how it is. We don't want to put young people under influence we haven't been careful with."

Under influence.

Lance heard the words through a lens that had already started forming. As though he were dangerous. As though he were some project. As though he had not been in this church his whole life.

"Sure," Lance said. He smiled, but the smile had no warmth in it.

By Monday morning, the phrase had grown teeth. *We don't want to put young people under influence we haven't been careful with.* He replayed it while brushing his teeth, while driving to work, while standing in the warehouse pretending to care about inventory numbers. By lunch, it had become something else: *Pastor doesn't trust me.* By dinner, it had become clearer: *They don't want me to serve unless I fit their mold.* By night, it had become a verdict: *They only care about control.*

It can happen that fast. A sentence becomes a suspicion. A suspicion becomes a pattern. A pattern becomes a story. And once the story begins preaching, everything else becomes an illustration.

That Wednesday, Lance showed up to church in jeans. Nice jeans. Clean. Dark. Not sloppy. But jeans. He knew it was not what he normally would wear to church, especially for someone who wanted to be involved. He knew because he had lived there long enough to know. No one had to hand him a printed code.

He wore them anyway. Not because he was making a statement, he told himself. He just wanted to be comfortable. But when a man says he is not making a statement and then watches carefully to see who notices, he is usually making one.

Pastor Graham did notice. He did not rebuke him. He did not embarrass him. He did not say anything in the hallway. But Lance saw the quick glance. Not long. Not dramatic. Just enough.

There it is, Lance thought.

He walked into the service already defending himself against a confrontation that had not happened.

The message that night was from 1 Peter. Pastor Graham preached about submission. Lance nearly laughed. Of course. He looked down at his Bible, but he was not reading. He was gathering evidence. Parents. Pastors. Authority. Standards. Submission. Same thing every time. The words of the sermon became background noise. The story in his head was louder.

Afterward, a friend named Jason caught him in the foyer. "You all right?"

"Yeah," Lance said. "Why?"

Jason shrugged. "You just seem irritated."

Lance looked around, lowered his voice, and said the sentence that made everything sound better. "I'm just thinking through some things."

Jason nodded. "Like what?"

"I don't know." Lance paused, not because he did not know, but because he wanted to say it carefully. "I just wonder sometimes how much of this is actually Bible and how much is just preference."

Jason glanced toward the auditorium. "What do you mean?"

"I mean, music. Dress. Standards. All of it. Sometimes it feels like if you don't check every box, you're basically treated like you're backslidden."

Jason did not say much. That bothered Lance. He had expected agreement, or at least curiosity. Instead Jason said,

"I get asking questions. But be careful, man. Sometimes people start asking questions because they want answers. Sometimes they start asking questions because they already know what they want to do."

Lance smiled tightly. "Right. So now asking questions is wrong too."

"That's not what I said."

"No, I know." Lance stepped back. "It's fine."

It was not fine.

By the time he reached his car, Jason had been added to the story. Not as a villain yet, but as one of them.

That night, Lance searched online. Not for the first time, but now he searched with purpose. He did not type, *What does the Bible teach about separation?* He typed, *church standards legalism.* Then, *KJV only cult.* Then, *why independent Baptist churches are controlling.* Then, *spiritual abuse modesty standards.*

The internet answered like a serpent with a thousand ready-made arguments.

Post after post. Video after video. Comment thread after comment thread. Some of it was foolish. Some of it was bitter. Some of it was filthy. Some of it was probably true in certain situations, because there are real abuses, real hypocrisy, real harshness, real people who have been wounded by real sin under the cover of religious language.

That made the whole thing more dangerous. The devil does not need every witness to lie. He just needs enough truth to help a man build the wrong case.

Lance read for two hours. By midnight, he was no longer thinking about holiness, Scripture, or his own heart. He was thinking in new words: control, manipulation, fear-based religion, man-made rules, toxic authority, cult-like behavior. He had not used most of those words a week earlier. Now they felt like keys. They opened doors inside him.

The next Sunday, every part of church looked different. The ladies singing special music looked restricted. The teenagers sitting together looked sheltered. The ushers looked like rule enforcers. The platform standards looked performative. The hymns sounded old. The preaching sounded narrow. The King James Bible in his lap suddenly felt less like a treasure and more like a badge he was expected to wear.

It had not changed. But he had.

The fence had become the problem.

And that was the real turn. The issue was no longer a song, a pair of jeans, a standard, or even a church preference. The issue was authority. Lance wanted the freedom to decide which boundaries mattered and which ones did not. And any voice that challenged him could now be dismissed with a better word: *control.*

Pastor Graham preached from Romans 12: *"Be not conformed to this world."* Lance heard fear. The congregation sang, "Take my life, and let it be consecrated, Lord, to thee." Lance heard control. His mother asked if he wanted to come over for lunch. Lance heard pressure. His father asked how he was doing. Lance heard interrogation.

By then, the story was working beautifully. It explained everyone. It protected itself from correction. If someone warned him, that proved they were controlling. If someone stayed quiet, that proved they were cold. If someone was kind, that proved they were trying to pull him back in. If someone asked questions, that proved they did not trust him. There was no way to reach the story from the outside, because the story had already assigned motives to everyone who might challenge it.

The next permission came on a Friday night, when a coworker invited him to a young adults event at another church across town.

"Totally different vibe," the coworker said. "You'd probably like it. Nobody's uptight. Good music. Real preaching. People actually act like they enjoy being there."

Lance laughed. "What's that supposed to mean?"

His coworker grinned. "You tell me. You're the one always talking about your church like it's a parole office."

Lance had not realized he had been doing that. But he had.

The event was easy to justify. It was church, after all. Not a bar. Not a club. Not some wild party. Church. That made the permission feel safe. He was not running into obvious wickedness. He was stepping into something that still used Christian words, Christian songs, and Christian language. That was why it worked so well. The fruit did not look like rebellion. It looked like relief.

He told himself he was just visiting. Just seeing what else was out there. Just trying to be fair. Just wanting to know whether the warnings he had grown up hearing were accurate.

Just.

There was that word again.

The first thing he noticed when he walked in was the sound. It was not the music his church would have used. Not close. Lights low, drums strong, guitars swelling, people singing with eyes closed. The feeling was undeniable, and Lance received the feeling almost as proof.

Lance felt something. That was undeniable. It felt warm. Emotional. Free. No one cared what he wore. No one knew his parents. No one knew what standards he had been taught. No one expected him to carry himself as an example. No one asked what Bible he used or what music he listened to.

He was anonymous. And anonymity can feel like grace when a man is tired of accountability.

After the service, several people welcomed him. They were friendly. Really friendly. Not fake. Not obviously carnal. They talked about Jesus, community, healing, authenticity, and getting away from shame-based religion. The preacher that night had said, "Some of you grew up in churches where the rules mattered more than people. But Jesus didn't come to give you rules. He came to give you relationship."

People clapped. Lance felt seen. He did not ask whether the sentence was true. He liked how it felt. That was enough.

On the drive home, he played the worship song again. Then again. Then louder. He imagined telling people at his church about it. He imagined their faces, their concern, their disappointment, their warnings. The whole thing played out in his mind before anyone had said a word. By the time he got home, he had already been persecuted in an imaginary trial and had already won.

Saturday morning, he posted a quote.

Sometimes freedom begins when you stop confusing man-made rules with God.

He stared at it for a while before hitting post. Then he did.

The likes came quickly. Not from many people at his church, but from others. Old friends. Coworkers. People who had left similar churches. A girl he knew from camp who now attended a very different kind of church commented, "This. So much this." Another wrote, "Proud of you for seeing it." Someone else said, "Legalism is a cage."

Then came the longer messages.

Bro, I've been through the same thing. Took me years to recover.

You're not crazy. Those places control people with fear.

Once you get out, you'll never go back.

Lance read every one. Each comment felt like confirmation. Not because they had examined his heart. Not because they had opened Scripture with him. Not because they knew his pastor, his church, his parents, or the actual facts. They confirmed him because they agreed with the story. And agreement feels like truth when a man is already decided.

By Sunday, Lance did not go to his church. He told his mother he was visiting somewhere else. The silence on the phone after he said it bothered him.

"What church?" she asked.

He told her.

She paused again. "Lance, be careful."

There it was. Careful. That word now sounded like fear.

"Mom, I'm not leaving God. I'm going to church."

"I didn't say you were leaving God."

"No, but that's what everyone acts like. Like if I don't do everything exactly the way our church does, I'm compromising."

"That's not fair."

"Maybe not. But it's how it feels."

That phrase had become very important to him: *how it feels.* It allowed him to speak with authority without proving anything.

He visited the other church again. Then again. Then he missed Wednesday at his own church because work had been long and he was tired. Then he missed the next Sunday night because he had plans. Then he missed soul winning because he had assignments due. Then he missed a workday because, honestly, he did not feel like walking back into all the looks.

The distance made the story easier to maintain. That is one reason distance is dangerous. It keeps correction from reaching the heart while the imagination keeps preaching.

Pastor Graham texted him after two weeks.

Hey Lance, missed you the last couple Sundays. Would love to grab coffee this week if you're free. Praying for you.

Lance stared at the message. It was kind. That annoyed him. It would have been easier if it were harsh. He waited six hours to reply.

Busy this week. Maybe sometime.

Pastor Graham answered:

No problem. I care about you. Door is always open.

Lance tossed the phone on his bed. *Door is always open.* It sounded manipulative to him. Everything did now.

That evening, he made another post.

Real shepherds don't control sheep. They feed them.

He almost deleted it. Then he thought of Pastor Graham's text and posted it.

This one got more attention. Someone commented, "Sounds like you escaped."

Escaped. That word had weight. He had not thought of himself that way. But he liked it.

A few church people saw the post. One older man messaged him privately and said, "Lance, I love you. Be careful about accusing people publicly. If there's an issue, go talk to Pastor directly."

Lance screenshotted the message and sent it to a friend from the new church.

See what I mean?

The friend responded:

Classic control. They always want private conversations so they can pressure you.

That settled it. Private conversation became dangerous. Public accusation became courage.

That is how backward a heart can get when the story owns the room.

The Word was getting loose too. Lance still used Bible language. More than ever, really. Grace. Liberty. Love. Spirit-led. No condemnation. Come as you are. All good words. But now they had been detached from other words: holiness, obedience, submission, separation, correction, doctrine, faithfulness.

He did not reject the Bible. He just started selecting which Bible words were allowed to speak.

At the new church, most people used different versions. That did not bother him at first. Then it began to feel refreshing. Easier. Less rigid. Less "tribal," as someone there put it. One night, the preacher used three different versions in one message. Lance noticed, then told himself not to be narrow.

The next week he ordered a new Bible. Not because he had studied the issue carefully. Not because he had searched the matter out with fear and trembling. He was tired of the old Bible being attached to the old guardrails.

So, when the new one arrived, he felt a strange thrill opening it. Like he had crossed a line.

Because he had.

Not simply because another version was now in his hands. The deeper issue was what the change meant in him. He was not reaching for clarity. He was reaching for distance. Distance from his parents. Distance from Pastor

Graham. Distance from the church that had raised him. Distance from the convictions that had once held him. Distance from the version of himself that still felt obligated to obey.

The new Bible became a symbol. One more old restraint crossed. No lightning fell. No immediate disaster came. That mattered to him.

See? That was the inner sermon. *Nothing happened.*

The warning had shrunk again.

Over the next few months, Lance's life loosened in stages. The music changed first. Then the clothes. Then the schedule. Then the friends. Then the language. Then the entertainment. Then the convictions he used to call convictions became "how I was raised."

He did not become wild. That almost made it harder to see. He still went to church most Sundays. He still posted verses. He still talked about Jesus. He still had spiritual conversations. He still said things like, "I'm closer to God now than I ever was." Maybe sometimes he even felt that way.

Feelings are powerful, especially when they are no longer being judged by truth.

The new church was full of motion, warmth, and emotion. Lance loved the music. He loved the atmosphere. He loved that nobody seemed worried about the things his old church had warned about. There were no awkward conversations about standards, separation, entertainment, or personal holiness unless they could be framed in the soft language of growth and healing. No one made him feel guilty.

That became his test for health. If he felt guilty, it was bad. If he felt accepted, it was good. By that standard, the new place was very good. By that standard, the old place was very bad.

It did not occur to him that guilt may be a mercy when the conscience is trying to stay alive.

Several months after he left, Lance drove past his old church on a Wednesday night. He had not planned to. There was construction on the main road, and the detour took him that way. The parking lot was full.

For a moment, he felt something he did not expect. Not anger. Not exactly sadness. Something closer to homesickness. He saw Mr. Dalton's truck. Mrs. Weaver's van. The church bus. Pastor Graham's car near the side door. He thought about being twelve years old, carrying a plate of cookies down the fellowship hall. He thought about teen camp. He thought about kneeling at the altar when God had dealt with him. He thought about the time Pastor Graham had driven forty minutes to visit him after his grandfather died. He thought about his father's hand on his shoulder during invitation. He thought about Scripture memory, hymns, workdays, laughter, conviction, safety.

For a few seconds, the story lost its grip. It had not all been control. It had not all been fear. It had not all been a cage. Much of it had been love. Imperfect love, yes. Sometimes awkward. Sometimes stricter than he understood. Sometimes mixed with human weakness, as all churches are. But love all the same.

Then his phone buzzed. A friend from the new church had sent a reel mocking "fundamentalist trauma." Lance watched the first three seconds. A man in a suit pretended to yell about skirt lengths while dramatic organ music played in the background. The comments were full of laughing emojis.

Lance laughed too. But not as freely as before.

He drove on.

A week later, his mother asked if he would come to dinner. He almost said no. Then he went. The meal was normal at first. His younger siblings talked too much. His dad asked about work. His mom had made roast, potatoes, carrots, and the rolls he liked.

After dinner, his father asked if they could talk.

Lance stiffened. "I figured this was coming."

His dad looked tired. Not angry. Tired.

"Son, I'm not here to fight with you."

"Okay."

"I just want to ask you something."

Lance leaned back as his father folded his hands on the table.

"What exactly did you leave?"

The question irritated him.

"My church."

"No," his father said gently. "I know where you stopped attending. I'm asking what you left in your heart."

Lance looked away.

His father continued. "Did you leave hypocrisy? Did you leave actual false doctrine? Did you leave because someone sinned against you and refused to make it right? Or did you leave a fence because you wanted the field on the other side?"

Lance's jaw tightened. "There it is."

"No, listen to me." His father's voice stayed quiet. "I'm not saying every standard is Scripture. I'm not saying every application has to be exactly the same in every church. I'm not saying pastors can't be wrong or parents can't be heavy-handed. But I am asking whether you went back to the Bible honestly, or whether you went online looking for people who would help you feel right."

Lance wanted to answer quickly. He could not.

His father said, "Son, if you search for permission, you'll find it. If you search for truth, it may cut you first."

The words landed. Lance hated that they landed. He said very little after that.

Driving home, he was angry. Then unsettled. Then angry again. The old pattern tried to help him. *Dad just doesn't get it. They're scared of losing control. They can't handle me thinking for myself.* But the words did not work as well this time.

What exactly did you leave?

The question followed him into his apartment. He sat on the edge of his bed and looked around the room. Clothes on the floor. A guitar in the corner. Laptop open. New Bible on the desk. Old Bible on the shelf, half hidden under a stack of notebooks.

For reasons he could not explain, he pulled the old Bible down. The cover was worn. His name was written inside in his mother's handwriting. A verse underneath. The pages had markings from camp, youth conference, revival meetings, private devotions, sermons that had once gripped him and changed him.

He turned to Proverbs without meaning to.

"My son, hear the instruction of thy father, and forsake not the law of thy mother."

He closed it too fast. Then opened it again. This time to Hebrews.

"Obey them that have the rule over you, and submit yourselves: for they watch for your souls…"

He did not want that verse. Not now. He turned somewhere else.

Romans.

"Be not conformed to this world…"

The old words were not dead. He was just farther away from them than he had admitted.

For the first time in a long time, Lance wondered whether the problem had not been that the church made everything too heavy. Maybe he had made obedience too light.

The thought scared him because if that were true, then the whole story had to be reexamined. Not every concern vanished. He still had questions. He still did not understand every standard. He still thought some people had been clumsy, and maybe they had. He still had things to work through. But another possibility had entered the room.

Maybe the fence was not the enemy. Maybe the fence had been protecting something. Maybe he had called it a cage because he wanted what was outside it.

Lance did not go back the next Sunday. Stories do not always collapse in one night. Sometimes they fight to live. But something had cracked.

The next time he saw a post mocking his old kind of church, he did not share it. The next time someone called them a cult, he did not join in. The next time he heard someone talk about freedom as though it meant no restraint, he felt that old verse press against him: *"use not liberty for an occasion to the flesh."*

He had forgotten that verse. Or maybe he had avoided it.

Two weeks later, Lance texted Pastor Graham.

Can we get coffee sometime?

The reply came within three minutes.

Absolutely. I'd be glad to.

Lance stared at the screen. No rebuke. No lecture. No "I told you so." Just an open door.

He almost cried. Not because everything was fixed. It was not. Not because he had all his answers. He did not. But because for the first time in months, he saw the door as mercy instead of manipulation.

At coffee, Lance talked more honestly than he expected. Not perfectly. Not humbly at every moment. He still defended too much. Still explained. Still softened. Still said "I just felt like" more often than he should have. But eventually, after circling the issue for nearly an hour, he said it plainly.

"I think I wanted out."

Pastor Graham waited.

Lance looked down at his cup. "I don't think I called it that. I called it questions. I called it freedom. I called it getting away from man-made rules. And maybe I do have some real questions. But I think underneath it, I wanted out from under the pressure. I wanted to stop feeling like there were lines everywhere."

Pastor Graham nodded slowly. "That's an honest place to start."

Lance swallowed. "I made you the villain."

Pastor Graham's face softened. "I know."

That answer hurt more than denial would have.

Lance looked up. "I'm sorry."

The words were small. But true.

The months that followed were not simple. Real growth rarely is. Lance had to sort through questions carefully, not as weapons but as a man under the Word. He had to apologize to his parents. He had to delete posts. He had to stop feeding on voices that loved his resentment more than his soul. He had to admit that some of what he had called discernment was just pride with better vocabulary.

And he had to learn the difference between a conviction and a standard. A conviction had to be settled before God from Scripture. A standard was a guardrail that helped protect obedience. The standard itself was not holiness. But tearing down every guardrail was not maturity. That was one of the hardest lessons, because the flesh hates guardrails until the wreckage comes.

Looking back later, Lance could see the Eden pattern more clearly than he could see it while he was inside it. The question had entered first: *Why does everything have to be such a big deal?* Then the authority became the villain: Pastor Graham, his parents, the church, the people who warned him. Then the one "no" took over: the standards, the music, the dress, the Bible issue, the fact that he could not serve on his own terms. Then the Word got loose: grace without holiness, liberty without caution, love without correction, questions without submission. Then the wrong thing started sounding reasonable: a looser church, fewer guardrails, a faith that asked less of him and affirmed more of him. Then judgment looked small. Nothing happened when he changed the music. Nothing happened when he missed church. Nothing happened when he posted publicly. Nothing happened when he started calling caution control.

But something had happened.

He had drifted. His appetite had changed. His confidence had grown while his obedience had weakened. He had not become free.

He had become easier to move.

That was what sobered him most.

The forbidden fruit had not been a bottle, a woman, or a bag of money. It had been permission. Permission to become the final judge of every restraint in his life. Permission to rename conviction as extremism, standards as control, pastoral warning as manipulation, and biblical correction as abuse. Permission to loosen, resent, redefine, and step away from the people and standards that had once helped guard him.

The serpent had not asked for his whole life at once.

Just the next permission.

And for a while, Lance had called that freedom.

Case File Three: The Next Permission

By the time Rachel saw the picture, she had already been tired for months.

Not tired in the dramatic way people talk about when they want sympathy. Not collapse-on-the-floor tired. Just worn thin. The kind of tired that settles behind the eyes and makes small things feel heavier than they are. The laundry was folded but still sitting in baskets. The kitchen island had become a migration route for school papers, cups, charger cords, unopened mail, and one lonely sock that seemed to have survived the flood by attaching itself to a grocery receipt. The kids had been arguing since breakfast. Someone needed new shoes. Someone else needed a permission slip signed. The baby had woken twice the night before, and her husband, Rick, had slept through both times like a man protected by divine anesthesia.

Rachel was standing in the kitchen, scrolling her phone with one thumb while waiting for the coffee to finish. That was when she saw it. A family from church had posted anniversary pictures. Not just a quick picture at dinner. A whole post. Matching smiles. A nice restaurant. Flowers. A long caption from the husband about how thankful he was for his wife, how she made their house a home, how he did not deserve her, how she was his best friend.

Rachel read it once, then read it again. Then she looked across the kitchen at Rick's travel mug still sitting by the sink, the one he had forgotten after saying he was already late. She shut the coffee maker off harder than necessary.

It was just a picture. That was all. But something had entered. Not a decision. Not a plan. Not even a full thought yet. Just a little question: *Is this what marriage was supposed to feel like?*

She hated that the question came so easily. She knew better. She knew social media was not real life. She knew people posted anniversaries, not arguments. She knew nobody uploaded the tired Thursday night after both spouses had nothing left and somebody still had to take out the trash. She knew all of that. But the question stayed, and once it stayed, it began finding places to sit.

That night, Rick came home late. Not terribly late. Just late enough. He had called ahead, said work ran over, said he was sorry. When he walked through the door, the kids rushed him like puppies, and he smiled, kissed the top of one head, tried to answer two questions at once, and set his bag on the chair instead of hanging it up.

Rachel saw the bag. Not the tired man. Not the hours he had worked. Not the pressure he carried. *The bag.*

Of course.

She was making dinner, and the youngest was pulling at her leg, and Rick said, "Smells good." It should have helped.

It did not. She wanted him to notice more than dinner. She wanted him to notice the day, the mess, the weight, her. She wanted him to walk in, take inventory of her soul, and somehow know exactly which words would lift the whole room. Instead, he said, "Smells good," and checked his phone.

The question moved again: *Is this all it is?*

By bedtime, Rachel had said very little. Rick could feel it, but he did not know what it was. He asked once, "Everything okay?" That was the moment. A door, maybe. But Rachel heard the question through the hurt already gathering in her mind. *Everything okay?* Was he serious? She gave the answer that punishes without technically lying.

"I'm fine."

Rick waited a second, unsure whether to press or retreat. He chose retreat. That became evidence.

By the next morning, Rachel was not thinking, *He probably does not know what I need.* She was thinking, *He does not care enough to ask.*

That is how the story began. Not with another man. Not with secret messages. Not with hotel rooms or lies or anything that would have sounded scandalous if spoken out loud. It began with comparison. A picture. A caption. A question. A tired woman. A husband who was imperfect, distracted, and human. And then the mind started preaching.

By Friday, Rachel had seen three more posts. One woman's husband had surprised her with a weekend away. Another had written about their "weekly date night."

Another couple had posted family pictures at sunset, everyone glowing like they lived in a different creation where children never spilled juice and husbands never forgot trash day. Rachel knew those pictures were curated. But knowing something in the head is not the same as resisting it in the heart.

She began to notice what Rick was not. He was not romantic. Not really. He was not emotionally aware. He was not a natural leader at home, at least not in the way she had imagined a leader would be. He did not pray with her as often as he should. He did not notice when she was drowning unless she was already underwater. He did not understand how lonely a woman could feel while surrounded by noise.

Some of those things were true. That was part of the danger. The serpent doesn't need a completely false situation. Sometimes one real frustration is enough. One real wound. One real immaturity. One real lack. Then the heart begins building a world around it.

Rick became smaller in Rachel's mind, and then darker. The things he did well began to fade. He worked hard. He loved the children. He was faithful. He came home. He was not cruel. He provided. He could be playful with the kids when he had energy. He had apologized over the years, awkwardly maybe, but sincerely. Those things were still true, but they no longer preached as loudly as the lack.

The one "no" had taken over. Not a literal no. Not one forbidden tree in the middle of a garden. But the life she did not have. The marriage she imagined. The tenderness she thought other women were receiving. The version of herself she believed she might have been if she had married differently, lived differently, chosen differently. That version began standing at the fence, and Rachel began staring at it.

She did her devotions, but quickly. She read the chapter, marked the box, and moved on. The words were there, but she was not really under them. Prayer became mostly sighing. Church became routine. She sang the hymns, but she was somewhere else. She listened to preaching, but only the parts that could be applied to Rick seemed to land. When the preacher spoke about husbands loving their wives, she felt vindicated. When he spoke about contentment, she thought of other women. When he spoke about bitterness, she thought, *I'm not bitter. I'm just tired.* When he spoke about faithfulness, she felt a little prick in her conscience.

She brushed it away.

Nothing was happening. That became one of her favorite comforts. *Nothing is happening.* She was not doing anything wrong. She was not texting another man. She was not planning to leave. She was not being unfaithful. She was just disappointed. Just lonely. Just honest about where things were.

That word *honest* became useful. It gave dignity to thoughts that should have been challenged. *I'm just being honest.* But honesty without submission can become its own kind of deception. A person can honestly describe a feeling and still be wrong to feed it. Rachel had not learned that yet. Or maybe she had learned it and did not want to remember.

Then, on a Tuesday afternoon, the opportunity came.

His name was Aaron Keller. She had not thought about him in years. He had been a friend from high school. Not quite a boyfriend. Not nothing either. One of those unfinished stories that nostalgia loves because it can be rewritten without consequences. He had moved away after graduation, married someone, had kids, and existed mostly as a name that occasionally appeared under a mutual friend's post.

Then he commented on one of Rachel's pictures.

Look at that crew. You haven't changed a bit.

Rachel smiled before she meant to.

It was harmless. That was the first word the flesh offered. *Harmless.* She liked the comment, closed the app, reopened it, read it again, and closed it once more.

That evening, while Rick helped one child with math and another cried over pajamas that apparently felt "too stripey," Rachel found herself thinking about Aaron's comment. *You haven't changed a bit.* Rick had not said anything like that in a long time. Not because he thought she had changed for the worse. Probably not. But because he did not say those things easily anymore. Or often enough. Or maybe at all.

Aaron had noticed. That was the thought. Aaron had noticed.

The next morning, there was a message.

Hey stranger. Your family is beautiful. Hard to believe we're old enough to have kids this big.

Rachel stared at it. There was still time to leave the tree. She could have deleted it. She could have shown Rick. She could have answered briefly and ended it. She could have said, *Hope you're doing well,* and left it there. She could have asked herself why the message felt warmer than it should have. She could have brought the little spark into the light before it had oxygen.

Instead, she typed:

I know. It's crazy. Feels like yesterday we were all at football games pretending we had life figured out.

She watched the three dots appear, and something in her woke up. Not something holy. But something alive.

Aaron wrote back quickly.

That's because we definitely did have life figured out.

Rachel laughed. Out loud.

Rick looked over from the table. "What?"

"Nothing," she said, turning the phone slightly. "Just something funny."

That was the first concealment. Small. Almost invisible. But real.

Nothing had happened, she told herself. And yet something had.

By the end of the week, they had exchanged several messages. Nothing openly sinful. Nothing that would have looked shocking if read in isolation. Old memories. Kids. Work. The strange feeling of getting older. A joke about high school hair. A comment about how fast life moves. But the messages had begun to occupy space. Rachel checked her phone more often. She wondered when he would answer. She smiled at phrases she would not have wanted Rick to read over her shoulder. She started carrying her phone with her into the laundry room. Then into the bathroom. Then turning it face down when she set it on the counter.

The smoke alarm was chirping.

She called it privacy.

By the next week, Aaron knew Rick was "not a bad guy, just not very present." Rachel knew Aaron's wife was "a good mom, but they had grown apart in a lot of ways." There it was. The forbidden thing had started preaching back.

We are not trying to do anything wrong. We are just both in hard places. It is nice to talk to someone who understands. No one is being inappropriate. This is just conversation.

Just. That word did a lot of work. Just talking. Just catching up. Just being honest. Just encouraging each other. Just a friend. But the thing about "just" is that it often appears when the conscience is already uncomfortable.

Rachel began comparing the men moment by moment. Rick came home tired, and Aaron sent a thoughtful message. Rick forgot to ask about her day, and Aaron remembered something she had said three days earlier. Rick fell asleep during a movie, and Aaron was awake at 11:37 p.m. with, *You ever feel like life turned out differently than you expected?*

Rachel stared at that one for a long time. *Yes,* she typed. Then deleted it. Then typed: *Sometimes.*

Aaron answered: *Me too.*

Two words. But they opened a room.

After that, the conversation changed. Not all at once. It just deepened in the way wrong things deepen when no one is willing to call them wrong yet. They talked about disappointment. Then marriage. Then loneliness. Then what they used to be like. Then how easy it was to lose yourself. Then how some people never really get seen.

Rachel began to feel known by a man who did not have to live with her, raise children with her, pay bills with her, disappoint her in ordinary ways, or love her through the daily friction of actual married life. Aaron was all conversation. That made him easy to admire. Rick had to be a husband in the kitchen, in the budget, in the minivan, in the discipline of children, in the exhaustion of Wednesday night, in the unromantic grit of ordinary faithfulness. Aaron only had to be a voice on a screen.

But Rachel was no longer weighing things honestly. Appearance had begun to preach. Aaron's words looked good for food. They fed something. They made her feel alive, seen, interesting, pursued. They were pleasant to the eyes. She looked at his profile pictures longer than she should have. She noticed the gray in his beard, the way he smiled, the way his family pictures felt less perfect than others and therefore more real. And they were desired to make one wise. Because now Rachel began to believe this was teaching her something: about herself, about what she needed, about what marriage should be, about how long she had been ignored, and about how maybe God did not intend her to spend the rest of her life emotionally starving.

That was when the Word began getting loose. Not absent. Loose. Rachel still knew what adultery was. She still knew marriage was sacred. She still knew vows mattered. She still knew what the Bible said. But now she handled those truths differently.

We have not crossed that line. God knows my heart. I've tried for years. A person can only be lonely for so long. Surely God does not expect someone to live dead inside.

And then the most dangerous one:

Once I figure this out, I'll get right with God.

That thought should have terrified her. It comforted her instead. She was no longer thinking like a woman under the Word. She was thinking like a woman trying to keep the Word nearby in case she needed it later.

Sunday morning, she sat beside Rick in church and sang with everyone else. Aaron had messaged her before the service. *Hope today is peaceful for you.* She had read it in the parking lot. Now, while the congregation sang, her phone sat in her purse like a small hidden fire.

The preacher read, *"Drink waters out of thine own cistern, and running waters out of thine own well."* Rachel felt heat rise in her neck. For one brief moment, the fog thinned. She saw it. Not all of it, but enough. She saw the messages. The secrecy. The emotional dependence. The way she had begun dressing a little more carefully before posting pictures. The way she had stopped praying honestly. The way Rick had become the villain because she needed him to be the villain. The way Aaron had become wise, kind, and safe because he existed outside the costly reality of marriage.

She saw enough to be afraid. Then the service ended, and fear faded. By Monday, the warning had shrunk again.

Everybody struggles. Lots of marriages go through this. I'm not the only one. People get divorced all the time and God still uses them. Besides, no one knows what it has been like.

That was not entirely false. People did get divorced. God did forgive sinners. Other marriages did struggle. Rachel's loneliness did matter. Rick did have things to answer for as a husband. But the heart can take true sentences and arrange them into a lie. That's one of the devil's oldest skills.

By Thursday, Aaron asked if she wanted to meet for coffee. Just to talk in person.

Rachel read the message while standing beside the dryer. The house was quiet. The kids were at school. Rick was at work. The dryer hummed behind her, rolling the family's clothes in warm circles while her thumb hovered over the screen.

This was a tree. Not the first one, maybe. Not even the first fruit. She had touched smaller branches already. She had lingered. She had listened. She had looked. She had let the forbidden thing become useful, beautiful, and wise in her imagination. But this was still a line. She knew it.

She set the phone down, walked away, came back, and read it again.

Aaron sent another message.

No pressure. I just think it would be good to see you.

Good. That word hooked itself in her mind. Good for whom? Good according to what? Good under whose voice? Rachel did not ask those questions. Not then.

She typed:

Maybe. I'd have to figure out when.

The next permission. That was all the flesh needed. Not the whole collapse. Just the next permission.

The days after that were strange. Rachel became both lighter and darker. Lighter because anticipation has a way of mimicking joy. Darker because secrecy has a way of eating the soul from the inside. She was kinder to Rick sometimes, which made her feel better about herself. Then colder other times, because his very presence complicated the story she needed to keep believing.

She began imagining conversations. With Rick: calm, tearful, brave. She would explain that she had been lonely for years. He would finally understand. Maybe he would even admit he had failed her. Maybe they would separate gently. The kids would be sad, of course, but children were resilient. Better two peaceful homes than one tense one. That phrase appeared from somewhere. She had heard it before. It sounded compassionate. It also helped.

With Aaron: honest, tender, restrained. They would not rush. They would do this "the right way," whatever that meant after doing the wrong thing long enough to need the phrase.

With God: later. She would come back later. Once everything settled. Once the dust cleared. Once she was happy enough to be spiritual again. That was perhaps the most frightening part. She had begun imagining repentance as a future accessory to disobedience, a thing she could put on afterward.

The coffee meeting happened on a rainy afternoon. Rachel chose a place across town. Not because she was hiding, she told herself. Just because it was quieter there. Less chance of running into people. Not that there was anything to hide. But still.

Aaron was already seated when she arrived. He stood when he saw her, and that small courtesy moved her more than it should have. They talked for an hour and a half. At first, it was nervous and ordinary. Then familiar. Then warm. Then dangerous.

He told her she looked beautiful.

She looked down, smiled, and said, "Don't."

But she did not leave. That was another line.

He apologized, but not really. "I'm sorry. I just mean it."

She should have hated that. She did not.

On the drive home, Rachel cried. Not because she was repentant. Not yet. She cried because she felt trapped between two stories. The old story: vows, children, church, duty, Scripture, faithfulness, endurance, repentance, truth. The new story: being seen, being wanted, being understood, being alive again. One of those stories was from God. The other sounded like salvation without a cross.

When she got home, Rick was making spaghetti. The kitchen was a wreck. One child was reading at the table. Another was lying on the floor for reasons no one understood. Rick looked up and said, "Hey. I started dinner. Figured you had a lot today."

Rachel almost broke. Almost. Because there he was. Not the villain. Not the obstacle. Not the flat character she had written into her private story. A tired man, trying awkwardly to love his wife by boiling noodles and burning the edges of garlic bread. For a moment, she saw him clearly.

Then her phone buzzed.

Aaron.

Today was good. Maybe too good.

Rachel turned the phone over quickly. Rick noticed. Not fully. But enough.

"You okay?" he asked.

There it was again. A door. This time, it was wider. Rachel could have stepped through it. She could have said, "No. I'm not. I need to tell you something before it gets worse." She could have dragged the serpent into the light. Instead, she said, "I'm just tired."

That night, the messages crossed a line neither of them could pretend not to see. Not physically. Not yet. But morally. Emotionally. Spiritually. Words were said that belonged inside marriage. Longings were admitted. Futures were hinted at. Boundaries were discussed only so they could be moved. They promised they would be careful, which was another way of admitting they were already in danger.

Rachel slept badly. The next morning, she did not read her Bible. She did not even pretend.

By then, the warning had become very small.

God will forgive. No one understands. This is complicated. I deserve to be loved. The kids will adjust. Rick will probably be happier too. We will handle this carefully. We are not bad people.

Sentence by sentence, the cost shrank.

Then came the afternoon Rick found the messages. Not all of them. Enough.

Rachel had left her phone on the counter while helping one of the kids find a missing library book. Aaron's name appeared on the screen. Then a line of preview text. Rick did not snoop. Not exactly. But he saw enough to feel the room tilt. When Rachel came back into the kitchen, he was holding the phone. His face had changed. Not angry first. Broken first.

"What is this?" he asked.

Rachel froze.

There are moments when the story collapses under the weight of another person's pain. This was one of them. For weeks, she had imagined Rick as dull, distant, careless, emotionally absent. But now he stood in front of her with tears in his eyes, and all the simple categories she had built began to fail. He was not a symbol. He was her husband. And she had wounded him.

She reached for the phone. "Rick, I can explain."

That was the old instinct. Cover. Manage. Arrange. Control the damage. But even as she said it, she knew the sentence was wrong. She could explain the timeline. She could explain the loneliness. She could explain the messages, the coffee, the frustration, the slow drift of her heart. She could explain Rick's failures too, and some of those explanations would be true. But explanation was not confession.

And for the first time in weeks, the Word of God came back not as a verse fragment to manage, but as light.

"He that covereth his sins shall not prosper..."

Rachel sat down. The room was quiet except for the hum of the refrigerator and one child laughing somewhere upstairs, still mercifully unaware that something terrible had entered the house. Rachel looked at Rick. Then at the phone. Then back at Rick.

"It's wrong," she said.

The words came out flat and shaking. Not polished. Not complete. But true.

"It's wrong. I have been wrong."

Rick closed his eyes.

She had thought confession would make her feel clean. At first, it made her feel exposed. That is what light does when a person has been hiding.

The days that followed were painful. Not movie-painful. Not dramatic in the way people imagine. Just awful. Slow. Humbling. Full of consequences that did not disappear because she finally told the truth. There were conversations. Tears. Questions she did not want to answer. Trust that had been cracked and could not be glued back together with one apology. A pastor brought into the matter. A phone number blocked. Social media deleted. Passwords shared. Counseling scheduled. Late-night prayers that felt more like groaning than speaking.

Rachel hated some of it. The flesh in her still wanted to soften the language. *It was emotional. We were just talking. Nothing physical happened. I was lonely. Rick had failed me too.* Some of that was true. But none of it changed what it was.

She had eaten enough fruit to know the serpent does not stay to help with the consequences.

Aaron did not have to sit across from Rick and watch his face. Aaron did not have to answer the children when the house felt strange. Aaron did not have to rebuild trust, confess sin to spiritual authority, or live under the weight of what had almost been destroyed.

Aaron sent one more message from a different account.

I'm sorry. I never meant for it to blow up like this.

Rachel stared at those words for a long time. *Blow up like this.* As though the problem were the explosion and not the fire. She deleted it. Then blocked him again and told Rick.

For the first time, it felt less like loss and more like sanity.

Months later, Rachel would still remember the beginning more than the end. Not because the end did not matter. It did. The end was where the pain became visible. The end was where the cost came due. But the beginning was where the war had actually been lost.

The picture online. The question. The comparison. The small resentment. The way Rick became the villain. The way another life began looking like freedom. The way Scripture became distant. The way warnings shrank. The way one message became one conversation, one conversation became one secret, one secret became one meeting, and one meeting nearly became the grave of her home.

That was what frightened her most afterward. Not that she had woken up one morning and wanted adultery. She had not. She had only wanted to be noticed. Then understood. Then admired. Then relieved. Then free.

The serpent had not asked for everything at once.

He had only asked for the next permission.

And nearly got the house.

Do Not Wait for the Fruit to Be in Your Hand

These stories are fictional, but the pattern is not. The movement should feel familiar because Eden still speaks.

A question enters. A boundary starts looking suspicious. The one who warned becomes the villain. The forbidden thing begins to glow. The Word gets loosened. The warning shrinks. The next permission starts looking harmless. And before long, a man is much farther down the road than he ever meant to go.

So, don't read these stories merely as stories. Read them as mirrors.

If nothing in them touched anything in you, then thank God and stay watchful. But if something caught—if some sentence felt uncomfortably close, if some thought sounded familiar, if some part of one of these stories felt like it had walked through your own mind—don't brush that away.

That may be mercy.

The issue is not whether you are as far down the road as Daniel, Lance, or Rachel. That's the wrong question. The better question is: *has the pattern started?*

Has the question entered? Have you been feeding a story? Have you turned the person who warned you into the villain? Have you started calling guardrails bondage? Have you been looking for voices that will give you permission? Have you been minimizing what God said would happen? Have you been telling yourself, "It's not that big of a deal," "I can handle it," "I'll get right later," or "This is different"?

If so, do not wait.

Do not wait until the fruit is in your hand. Do not wait until the marriage is broken, the church is left, the bitterness is rooted, the secret is exposed, the children are wounded, the conscience is dulled, or the damage is done.

Break the pattern early.

Stop the conversation. Return to the Word. Drag the story into the light. Talk to the person you have turned into the villain. Get away from the tree. Remove the pipeline. Confess what needs to be confessed. Ask for help before pride turns a warning into an accusation.

And do not call that extreme. Call it biblical.

The Bible does not speak softly about danger. It says *flee. Abstain. Mortify. Crucify. Make no provision for the flesh.* Those are not decorative words. They are rescue words.

The serpent never asks for everything at first. He asks for the next permission.

So, don't give it to him.

If Eden teaches us anything, it teaches us that the battle is often lost in the mind before the hand ever moves. But by the grace of God, it can also be interrupted there: at the question, at the story, at the first resentment, at the first secret message, at the first loosened conviction, and at the first moment when God's clear Word starts feeling negotiable.

That's where the pattern must be broken.

The serpent still speaks. He still questions what God has said. He still makes the restriction look cruel, the warning look small, and the forbidden thing look wise. But God has already spoken, and the safety of the soul is found in staying with His voice.

That's where the Eden study closes. But the enemy's recorded words do not end in the garden. In the next book, we'll go to Job, where another weapon speaks.

Accusation.

ONE LAST WORD

Friend, if you've read this far and you don't know for sure that you're saved, don't close this book without settling it. Life is short, eternity is long, and Christ has already paid the price for your sins on the cross.

The Bible says, *"Behold, now is the accepted time; behold, now is the day of salvation."* (2 Corinthians 6:2) Don't put it off. Don't wait for a better time. There may not be one.

Right now, turn from your sin and trust Jesus Christ alone as your Saviour. Call upon Him in faith, and He will save you.

That's His promise.

www.ingramcontent.com/pod-product-compliance
Lightning Source LLC
LaVergne TN
LVHW010659110826
845149LV00014B/3170

* 9 7 9 8 9 9 3 1 4 4 6 7 2 *